# THE FINEST KIND

# THE FINEST KIND

## The Fishermen of Gloucester

*by*

KIM BARTLETT

*photographs by*

NUBAR ALEXANIAN

W·W·NORTON & COMPANY· INC·

*New York*

Published simultaneously in Canada by George J. McLeod Limited,
Toronto. Printed in the United States of America.

All Rights Reserved

First Edition

This book was designed by Jacques Chazaud
Typefaces used are Bodoni and Bodoni Ultra Italic
set by Haddon Craftsmen, Inc.
Printing & Binding by Haddon Craftsmen, Inc.

Library of Congress Cataloging in Publication Data

Bartlett, Kim
  The finest kind.

  1. Fishermen—Massachusetts—Gloucester—Biography.
2. Gloucester, Mass.—Biography. I. Title.
SH20.A1B37   1977     338.3'72'7097445     77–8800
ISBN 0–393–08797–2

1 2 3 4 5 6 7 8 9 0

*To Tudy, Dirk, and Jake—with thanks*

# Contents

# Preface

Late one May night I was in the galley of the Gloucester dragger *Judith Lee Rose* talking with the mate, Dick Tucker. We were fishing off Corsair Canyon, about 180 miles to the southeast of Gloucester. We had just spent six straight hours on deck mending the net. For the third consecutive day we were socked in by a thick fog, the sea was sloppy, the men were tired. We'd been out five days with at least another five ahead of us before coming in, and the fish were obviously elsewhere. As we drank the stale, too often warmed coffee before going to our bunks, Dick said, "If you're going to write about fishermen, write about us, not about the old days."

"Finest kind," I answered.

I didn't need Dick's admonition. Kipling had handled that end eighty years earlier (it is said that his sole on-location research consisted of a schooner ride from Boston to Gloucester during which he was seasick most of the time), and since then there had been *nothing* more written about the fishermen—curious absence and in its way an insult to the men who still go down to the sea in ships and still confront the treachery and the drudgery involved in hauling a living from the ocean.

The "boats of wood" are now also of steel, their lines less aesthetic, their quarters more relaxing. But the "men

9

of iron" still fish them. Of that I was convinced, and after many months of being a lubberly member of a number of crews I can write with confidence that the fishermen are still the finest kind.

# *Acknowledgments*

Without hesitation, to the fishermen of Gloucester. There were some who were skeptical of my proposed book, and there were some who were skeptical of anyone who had the time to write one, when, they imagined, he should be earning an honest day's pay. (One crew was certain that I was a spy for the Internal Revenue Service.) But at no point were any of these less generous or open than those crews who made me feel, for the time I was with them, like one of their own.

And there were others—non-fishermen—without whose support and criticism I would never have made it past page one: David Cohen, who told me to rewrite or find something else to do; Quincy and Tatty Bent, who told me to keep writing and not do anything else; Nubar Alexanian, whose camera and enthusiasm were incentives; Stan and Ruthanne Collinson, who filled a painful breach; Peter and Jane Davison who never stopped asking, "How's it coming?" and gave a damn that it got done; and my wife, Tudy, who kept sending me back to the attic.

To all of them, fishermen and non-fishermen, finest kind.

11

# Cast of Characters

## AFLOAT

*St. Providenza*—length, 48 feet; built 1924 in Amesbury, Mass.
Thomas Aiello
Anthony "Nutzie" Aiello
Billy Aiello

*Cigar Joe II*—length, 45 feet; built 1947 in Port Clyde, Me.
Sebastian "Busty" Frontiero
Samuel Frontiero

*Linda B*—length, 57 feet; built 1949 in Quincy, Mass.
Rosario "Salvi" Testeverde
Joseph Testeverde
Thomas Frontiero

*Clinton*—length, 62 feet; built 1925 in Thomaston, Me.
Spava Bertolino

*Sea Buddy*—length, 35 feet; built 1929 in Fairhaven, Mass.
Anthony "Olly" Palazola

*Maureen*—length, 46 feet; built 1946 in Newport, R.I.
Santo Militello
Mike Orlando
Matteo Grappo
Anthony Militello

*Joseph & Lucia III*—length, 91 feet; built 1968 in Dorchester,
Mass.

    Gaetano "Tommy" Brancaleone
    Antonio "Tony" Brancaleone
    Giuseppi "Joe Charley" Brancaleone
    Gaspare Palazzolo
    Santo Aloi
    Gilbert Roderick


# ASHORE

Joe Favazza—*manager of Fishermen's Wharf*
Johnny LaTassa—*bartender at the House of Mitch*
Sammy Frontiero—*fisherman*
Chubby Loiacano—*fisherman*
Booty Loiacano—*fisherman*
Philly Verga—*fisherman*

# PART I

## The Inshore Fleet

# 1

---

## *Leaving the Harbor*

$I$t's black dark. The predawn chill settles a slick of dew on the hoods of cars parked along the street. A homemade hockey goal lies fallen on the curb. Houses in a row with opaque windows; in some, shades are pulled. A garbage pail rattles . . .

. . . And for the 6,543rd time in his life Tommy Aiello of the fishing dragger *St. Providenza* snaps off the alarm, shudders, and draws himself carefully out of bed, not disturbing his sleeping wife. He shuffles to the window and squints at the parking lot lights at the Tavern. They are bright and clear. He allows himself a shiver of disappointment. The fog that has socked in the harbor for the past two days has lifted. He stares at a sheet of newspaper lying on the parking lot. It lies there. There does not seem to be a trace of wind. The last hope dies stillborn in Tommy's slowly wakening mind. He's got to get dressed, Nutzie will be waiting. What a goddamned life!

* * *

The black plastic tag on the breast pocket of her simple, homely, pink and white uniform says the girl's name is Chris. She is sun-blonde and sun-beet tan, and her face is

17

flushed and fresh. She speaks quietly, warmly to the fishermen as they arrive at Dunkin' Donuts at four in the morning, sleep dazed and heavy footed, lumber to a stool, slouch elbows down on the counter, and grumble, "A regular and a donut . . . I don't care, give me any donut."

Busty Frontiero and his brother Sammy of the *Cigar Joe II* are at the first two stools by the cash register. They've been there fifteen minutes already and hardly a word has passed between them. The two cups of coffee in front of them are nearly stone cold. Absentmindedly, Busty stirs his coffee back and forth. Sammy draws a cigarette from the breast pocket of his checkered shirt, lights it, slowly places the match in the saucer, and takes a long pull, letting the smoke drift from between his lips at its pleasure. Sammy stares at the rows of donuts. Busty watches Chris.

A few stools down is Olly Palazola of the *Sea Buddy*. Olly has a hangover from a cribbage game the day before at the House of Mitch down on Rogers Street. What else was there to do? The fog was so thick you couldn't see the breakwater, so there was no sense going out. How do you fish if you can't see the marks on shore? So he'd been suckered into the game with Kenny and Chubby and some other guy he didn't know, and not only had he drunk too much, he'd lost $50. And wasn't the old lady ripped when he got home for supper and he'd told her to shove it, and told the kids, too, and had tossed up the whole day in the toilet and gone to bed—and then had to take her car this morning because he'd done something to his, it wouldn't start, and what was that going to cost?

And now this Giovanni Gicalone is nagging at him in a torrent of bad Sicilian and indescribable English about some scheme Giovanni has to convert his scunga-bunga dragger and go longlining for swordfish.

Aie! This Giovanni! What he doesn't know about fishing! You can't go after swordfish in a boat like that. Mother of Jesus, the thing has already crashed into the Blynman Bridge twice because the reverse gear doesn't work. You got no room for the fuel you gotta have. You gotta be gone a week, two weeks. Where you gonna sleep? What happens, it gets bad out there? That old boat, Giovanni, she can't do that no more. Minga!

But Giovanni, weatherworn and wrinkled, short and stocky and dressed all over in oil-stained gray, is oblivious. And Olly, patient now to a fault, sips at his coffee which he nestles in his two thick-fingered hands, and listens and listens and shakes his head and listens some more and thinks to himself, "A man has to be starving to talk like this."

A car's headlights reflect through the plate-glass window facing on the vacant A&P parking lot. There's a creak, slam, click of a door closing. Busty turns around, squints, turns back to Sammy, mumbles something to him. Sammy straightens up, taps his cigarette pack deeper into his shirt pocket, takes a final sip of the cold coffee, and waits.

Tommy comes in and goes straight to the take-out counter. As ever, he is wearing a loose green workshirt and the tails hang over loose green pants, and he has on a black baseball cap set squarely on his round head. He has not shaved. He looks around, nods at Busty, Sammy, sees Olly, nods at him, and orders three cups of coffee and six donuts to go.

Busty and Sammy stand up. Sammy stretches, shakes himself, wipes a breaking yawn from his long, leathery face. Olly quickly finishes his coffee, takes out enough change to pay for both his and Giovanni's coffee, slides it on the counter. Giovanni says, "No, no," but Olly raises his hand, it's O.K.

The four men stand beside Tommy's old secondhand Chevy.

"Your engine fixed?" Tommy asks Busty.

"Seems all right. How d'ya know? How's yours?" Busty asks Olly.

"She goes. I gotta go easy, that's all. I still gotta straighten that rudder shaft. I don't know what's a matter. I get it so's it looks good, but she don't steer right. I gotta haul the boat. Next week, maybe," Olly answers. "Where you going today?"

"I don't know. Thacher's? I don't know. Nowhere's good. Doggies everywhere. Wha'd'ya do," Tommy says.

"I'm thinking HalfHour," Busty says. "There's always something there. What about the Bay?"

"Chubby says he got fish in the Bay. I don't know. Spava says he got two bags a doggies off HalfHour, but that's Spava. You don't know," Tommy says.

"I'll try Long Beach again," Olly says. "Four boxes a gray sole there Monday. As long as they hold, I'm not complaining. I don't like it too far out. She comes up thicka fog and I got no radar, I'll have a fuckuva time getting back in."

"Yeah, well, I don't know. Probably should stay in anyway. We lose money going out, there's no fish. . . . What about those prices outa New York? Minga! Nothing!"

"The fucking greasers, they don't give a shit. The stuff they catch. Trash. Little babies. It don't mean nothing to them. And it all goes to New York. We give those bastards quality fish, they give us nothing. The greasers give them shit, a lota shit, and they get the price. I'll tell youse, this fucking business is going downhill." Tommy is waking up.

"Yeah, well, I don't know. We're not making any money here, though," says Busty.

\* \* \*

Along the waterfront the fishermen are pulling themselves out of their cars, two men here, one there, some with brown paper bags filled with a Thermos of hot coffee and a sandwich, others with a loaf of Italian bread and packages of cold cuts.

They don't talk to each other. It is still too early, too dark. They walk wrapped in sleep. They are stiff, their backs hurt. They trudge down the separate wharves—Fisherman's Wharf, Felicia Oil, Frontiero Bros., Morse & Sibley's, A.D.E., Star Fishery's—their backs to the city, before them the placid inner harbor and the draggers, floating in ones and pairs, swing softly on lines made fast to the sturdy oak pilings supporting the wharves.

The men stand before the worn, oil-scummy ladders waiting for the man in front to make his way cautiously, hand below hand, foot below foot, down to the rail of the silent dragger below, waiting for him to turn around and catch the brown bag with the Thermos, the loaf of Italian bread, the packages of cold cuts. Then they follow down the ladder.

It's a routine. It seldom varies from crew to crew, boat to boat. For Salvi Testeverde and the *Linda B* it happens at 3:30 A.M. because Salvi fishes the Isle of Shoals and he wants to be there as dawn breaks. He wants his nets in the water before anyone else. Salvi is not greedy, just possessive. The Isle of Shoals is his fishing ground; the rest of the ocean belongs to anyone who wants it.

Spava Bertolino takes the *Clinton* out around 4 A.M.

He's been known to leave earlier, sometimes later, but usually it's 4 A.M. Spava will fish where the rest of the men fish. He'll have his nets overboard before almost anyone else and he'll haul them back about the same time the others do, and he'll come in when they do and maybe he'll catch the same as they have. Every day is another day for Spava. "I don't complain," Spava complains.

*   *   *

A "greaser" is a fisherman who was born in Sicily. Santo Militello is a "greaser." Tommy, Busty, Olly, Salvi, and Spava are not. Their fathers were. The distinction is important. Olly puts it this way:

"These guys fish like our fathers did—hard. They've known starvation. They know what it's like to have nothing on the table. Us? We've always had full bellies. These guys are always hungry. Fishing is their whole life. For us, it's a living. That's it."

But today Santo is late because, well, some friends came by last night and stayed awhile. Normally Santo would have been in bed by 10:30 or 11 P.M. at the latest. (With three teenage kids in the house, how do you sleep before then? So you gotta go to work, but it's their house, too.) But with the shrimp boycott on there's not that much big money being made fishing. You can get up early for shrimp, but for whiting? for what cod and haddock you're going to find? No one gets rich on groundfish.

Santo is philosophic. "We start late, we fish late. We get our day in." So instead of working from 3 A.M. until 4 P.M., it will be 4 A.M. to 5 P.M. or maybe 6 P.M. Might as well get the extra sleep now; the boycott can't last much longer. Too many people are losing money.

They walk down the recently renovated Felicia Oil
Wharf, Santo in the middle, short, solid, strong, compact.
He looks his forty-three years, no more. The tall, angular
man beside him is Mike Orlando. He walks slightly bent
over at the waist. He has on a black baseball hat which
peaks at the top. On the other side is Matteo Grappo, an
older man, shorter than Santo, a face set by years of fishing
into a dauntless expression in which surprise has long since
ceased to have a part. Mike and Matteo are "greasers."

And beside Matteo is Santo's son Anthony, fifteen years
old, lithe, and barely awake. Anthony carries a large bag
jammed with fresh Italian bread and hunks of Provolone.
Anthony is not a "greaser." That may be why he dreams of
someday playing professional hockey.

They reach the edge of the wharf. The tide is up so they
grab hold of the wheelhouse roof and swing, one after the
other, down onto the rail, then to the deck.

The dragger *Maureen* is western rigged with her wheelhouse before the deck like a lobster boat. The mast is set
aft of the wheelhouse, and from it hangs a block and tackle
and from the tackle hangs the net which the day before had
been hauled up to dry.

Anthony slacks the net to the deck, unhitches the the
tackle, makes it fast to the mast, then hauls the net toward
the starboard gunwale. Santo and Matteo go below to the
small forecastle, Matteo to the galley stove where he puts
on the coffee water, Santo into the engineroom where he
checks the oil, then returns to the wheelhouse and fires up
the diesel below. The boat first shakes, then relaxes into a
quiver. Santo races the engine, then slows it and steps out
on the deck and watches Mike free the lines fore and aft.

Mike nods, everything is clear. Santo returns to the
wheelhouse, throws the helm to starboard, puts the gear in

reverse, eases the throttle forward. The *Maureen* edges out of the slip between Felicia Oil and Frontiero Bros. The bow of the offshore dragger *Little Al* juts past the corner of the Felicia Oil Wharf, and lying in front of Frontiero Bros. is the sunken hull of the *Carlo & Vince*. There is a circle of floats anchored around the *Carlo & Vince* to contain the refuse that works loose from the deck and rises to the surface.

Santo squeezes the *Maureen* between the *Little Al* and the ring of floats. He heaves the helm to port, reverses the engine, increases the speed. The bow comes around under the point of the *Little Al;* the rush of water from the suddenly reversed propellor pushes in the ring of floats. The *Maureen* gains headway. Santo turns off the deck lights, flicks on the radar.

Anthony goes below and stretches out on the only empty bunk and falls into a heavy sleep. Like the *Acme* two hours before, the *Linda B* a half-hour earlier, the *Clinton* in a few minutes, the *St. Providenza, Cigar Joe II,* and *Sea Buddy* in half an hour; like the *Santo Lucia, Vince & Josephine, St. Bernadette, St. John II, Alba, Gigalone C, Little Flower, Baby Jerry, Cape Cod, Maria Virginia,* and the rest of the inshore fleet, Santo makes for the buoy off Ten Pound Island, locates the channel to the Dogbar Breakwater on the radar, sees that there are no other boats ahead, and pushes the throttle to three-quarter speed.

Mike stands in the stern and watches Ten Pound Island fall away. He reaches for a white plastic bucket tucked neatly among the stack of gray fiberglass shrimp boxes, grabs hold of the lanyard fastened to the wire handle, and drops it overboard, letting it fill a quarter up before hauling it back on board. He drops his pants and sits on it. When he's through, he pours it over the rail, fills it, swishes it, pours it out, fills it full, and washes down the deck, cleaning away what scraps may remain from yesterday's fishing. He replaces the bucket and comes forward to the wheelhouse and stands in the gangway, leans on the shelf running above it, and stares out at the flat, black sea and the light at the end of the breakwater now passing to port.

Matteo appears at the foot of the ladder with two white enamel mugs of hot coffee. Mike takes them both, passes one to Santo and keeps the other. Santo sips at his, flicks off the radar, checks his compass bearing. Mike finishes his coffee in three gulps and goes below, pushes in beside Anthony, and, lying on his back, his long arms laid out along his side, closes his eyes and is instantly asleep.

Santo gives a final look at the compass, adjusts the course, nods to Matteo, turns around and climbs onto the low bunk in the wheelhouse, curls himself into a tuck, and falls asleep.

Matteo takes over the helm, checks the compass, takes a sip of coffee, puts the cup back on the shelf, checks the compass, corrects the course . . .

In the twenty minutes it has taken the crew of the dragger *Maureen* to move from their cars to the boat, to get the boat away and past the breakwater and on course for Middle Bank, not one word has been spoken.

# 2

---

# *Setting Out*

Salvi Testeverde is fuming. Ever since coming out of the Annisquam River into Ipswich Bay he's been staring at the radar in front of him, and he's finally spotted what he suspected he was going to find—a white dot which has to be the dragger *St. John II,* and, goddamn it, the guy is in front of him, way in front, at least an hour, and, sonuvabitch, he's headed right for the Isle of Shoals.

"I shoulda gone earlier," Salvi mutters. "I knew it. I knew the guy'd be coming out here. Sonuva*bitch.*"

Salvi reaches behind him for the binoculars which are hanging by the depthfinder, rips them out of their case, slams the wheelhouse door open, and, balancing himself against the frame of the door, leans out and stares into the lightening black and tries to bring the *St. John II* into focus.

"Can't see shit," Salvi grumbles, "but it has to be him."

Salvi is a man of intense fury and serenity, one of those fishing captains for whom fishing is a daily battle between himself, the ocean, and the fish. He stands alone at the helm of his aging dragger, massive shoulders, broad, deep chest, heavy arms, and strong, thick-fingered hands, his head large and square, his face weathered and red, thick, tightly curled, graying white hair, his eyes hard with deep-set crow's-feet, his legs planted firmly against the roll, defiant at this thing which has gotten in *his* way and, *goddamn it,* it's going to get out of *his* way.

The trouble is, there's nothing Salvi can do about the *St. John II* except grumble. The guy got the early-morning jump and that's all there is to it. The *Linda B* won't move a knot faster no matter how many goddamns and sonsuvbitches he hurls.

Still, aside from his possessive attitude toward the Isle of Shoals (a few years ago, he tried to drive Busty from the grounds by dumping fish heads and entrails in Busty's path), Salvi's anger has a practical base. The last two days the inshore fishing grounds have been socked in with thicka fog. It has been impossible to fish because the fog blocked from view all the landmarks the fishermen need in order to tell where they are, where they should turn, where the wrecks are, where the hard or rough bottom that can rip up the nets is. With no fishing, the whiting have had a respite; they've been free to school together. There have been no nets cutting back and forth through them, scattering them all over the grounds.

Salvi knows that the first boat to the grounds is going to get the first tow through the fish, that it will be able to choose the best line on which to make the tow, and all that adds up to money. By the time he reaches the grounds the fish will be broken up. He'll be lucky to make a day's trip.

"God*damn* it," he yells, pacing back and forth across the wheelhouse, grabbing at his mug of lukewarm coffee, slugging it down, taking up the binoculars, and peering through the dark again. "Shit!"

\* \* \*

The *St. Providenza* is the oldest dragger in the fleet. She was built in Amesbury in 1924 and has been owned, captained, and crewed by Aiellos since she came off the ways, and, much to Tommy's unhappiness, she'll be fished by Aiellos until the day another coat of paint no longer holds her together.

She's been a good boat, a loyal boat. She's caught a lot of fish in her time, and old Joe Aiello, Tommy's father, was respected among the fishermen as a man of "class," a man who knew his fishing, fished hard, and did right by his family. He was a generous man who willingly shared what he knew with other fishermen, and back in his day such a man was rare.

Joe was rare in another way. He felt that fishing wasn't everything; that if you were going to have a family, you had to do more than make it and provide for it. Joe even went so far as to say, "I want to see my dog grow up."

So in the 1950s when he had the *St. Providenza* rebuilt for her thirtieth birthday, he insisted that the bunks be taken out of the forecastle "so that no one would ever be tempted to take her out overnight." From that point on the *St. Providenza* became strictly a day-fishing boat.

Today she is fifty years old and, as befits her age, she has become a fair-weather, day-fishing boat. She rides at the dock like a proud old lady. Her lines are straight and simple. She is painted a dark green with sedate gray trim. The only giddiness about her is a bright-orange deck which she bears because it is a Coast Guard regulation that the draggers have orange decks. It makes them easier to spot at sea from the air in case of emergency. She does not carry herself, for instance, the way Spava Bertolino's *Clinton* does. The *Clinton,* only one year her junior, is pristine white with baby-blue trim and an orange deck, and the boat is rusting out

29

and falling apart and is certain to reach her end long before the *St. Providenza*.

But when the seas blow up at all the *St. Providenza* stays in, and when winter fishing season comes her gear is stowed away, her lines made double-fast, and she goes into hibernation until spring.

And that suits Tommy fine, for if there is one thing Tommy hates it is fishing and he does it as rarely as possible.

Tommy is a mystery. No one knows how he supports his wife and five children. When all the boats are out, Tommy is often in. When he does go out, he is usually last out and often the first in. He is the last to get started in the spring and the first to tie up in the fall, and, unlike most of the other men who try to fish in the winter when the weather is fair, Tommy is at home living on "social" (unemployment).

Still, when he fishes, he's a good fisherman. They say there is very little about fishing he doesn't know and, like his father, he is generous with his knowledge. He knows his nets, he knows his bottom, he knows his marks. When his gear isn't fishing well, he is as capable as the best fishermen of running through all the possible problems, of calculating the speed of the boat, the length of the wires, the size and weight of the doors, the depth of the net, the number of meshes per square on the net, the number of floats on the headline, the number of weights on the footline, and determining, after all that figuring, that the reason he isn't catching fish is that the brace on the doors is a half an inch too low and this is throwing the balance off, causing them to dig in and not pull out to widen the mouth of the net.

And so Tommy will raise the height of the brace and the next day the gear will be fishing badly in another way and the calculating will begin again. Those who don't really understand Tommy say, "He fucks with his gear too much." Those who appreciate him say, "He doesn't have the heart for this business. He knows a lot, but he don't learn nothing."

Tommy stands in the wheelhouse, leaning against the jamb of the starboard door, one hand lightly on the helm; with the other he feeds the rest of his second donut into his mouth. In the distance to port are the twin lights on Thacher Island. The two towers are gradually taking shape, as are the white houses along the back shore. The horizon to the east begins to lighten as the black cover of night pulls back, revealing here and there black specks.

"Will you look at those guys. Wha'd'ya have to do to make 'em understand it doesn't do any good to get out so early. You gotta give the fish time to settle on the bottom. They gotta get down before you can catch 'em. You gotta wait till the sun comes up."

Tommy's brother Nutzie nods blankly. Nutzie (which is short for Anthony and whom Tommy affectionately calls "Nunu") is seated on the end of a narrow bench which runs along the port side of the wheelhouse. He is hunched over, barely awake. He has a cup of Dunkin' Donuts coffee wedged between his knees. Nutzie is the chief engineer and the first mate and the crew. Like Tommy he does not care much for fishing, but every time he decides to quit he feels guilty. If he doesn't fish with Tommy, who's going to? For everybody knows Tommy doesn't make money.

Behind Nutzie, curled up in a ball and sound asleep, is Nutzie's fifteen-year-old son Billy. A quarter-eaten donut lies loose in his right hand. He was dead to the world before the boat left the inner harbor.

"You know what happens? Some guy can't sleep, so he

says, 'What the hell, I might as well go fishing.' So he gets up an hour early and goes out. The boys see him out there and say to themselves, 'Jesus Christ! How'd he get out here so early?" So the next day they're all out. Well, the first guy sees this so's he's got to come out even earlier, and pretty soon they're coming in, having supper, and going out again. They're crazy. Wha'd'ya want to kill yourself like that for?"

"Yeah," says Nutzie. "I don't know." He finishes his coffee, tosses the empty cup through the door, takes out a cigarette, leans back against the wall of the wheelhouse, lights it, and lets a wave of smoke out. "I don't know."

* * *

GLOUCESTER DRAGGER *Cigar Joe II* TO GLOUCESTER DRAGGER *Sea Buddy:*

*Hello. Hello, Olly. Can you hear me, Olly?*

*Yeah, that's good, Busty. That's good. Where are you, Busty? Come in.*

*Just past the breakwater now, Olly, heading . . . hold a minute . . . heading east-by-southeast. I don't see you, Olly. Come back.*

*Yeah, well, Busty, I see you now. Who's that with you, 's that Tommy?*

*No, the* Cape Cod.*Tommy's not with you? I thought he'd left. Well, well. . . . Olly, you staying at Long Beach?*

*Yeah, Busty, I'll try it again today. I'll take a tow through here. I don't get nothing, maybe I'll tow down to the southard. You fishing to the southward?"*

*I don't know. There's nothing offa Thacher's. I was up there Monday. Nothing. A lotta dogs, some pinhead whit-*

*ing. I don't know. Gotta make some money. Anybody out
there with you?*

*A bunch of 'em up to the northeast. Can't tell who. You
seen Spava?*

*No, I guess he went out early. I didn't see his boat. I
don't know where he is. The Bay? I don't know. . . . Well,
well. . . . I'd better get the deck cleared. Think I'll set out
in a few minutes.*

*Yeah, he's probably in the Bay. . . . Well, yeah, Busty,
guess I'll be setting out pretty soon now. We'll see what
happens. Maybe I'll see you in the afternoon, things don't
look good up here.*

*That'll be good, Olly. I don't see you, I'll see you at the
barn.*

*You buying, Busty?*

*Let Tommy buy. He can afford it. He's a rich man.*

*Yeah, Busty, that's right. . . . Well, I gotta get ready.*

*O.K., Olly, us, too.*

* * *

The sun is rising. The ocean is flat and dark. The sky
is a black canvas lightly stippled with stars. Gradually the
ocean turns grey and the sky, black overhead, descends
toward the eastern horizon in ever-lighter shades of blue
until just above the horizon appears a long, narrow border
of gray. Yet, even in the gray, stars shine. Then the border
widens and widens and the stars disappear and the grey is
tinged with pink, and in the pink and gray come whisps of
red. And overhead the black is now dark blue and the water
is turning blue and at the far edge of the ocean the sun
appears, just the tip. Ever so slowly, it climbs over the edge

into the slight haze that until then was not noticeable. The haze swells the sun making it wooly and soft. Then the sun climbs over the haze and hardens into a ferocious red ball before which night has no challenge and so quickly hauls itself in and disappears to gather strength for its evening return. And the sun takes over the sky. Sparkles ride on the tops of waves.

\* \* \*

Santo rolls over on his back, stretches his legs out, puts his hands under the back of his head, and stares up at the low, white ceiling of the wheelhouse. He lowers his eyes and looks out the port window at the sun. He turns his head toward the near corner where an inexpensive alarm clock sits firmly in a homemade wooden holder. It is 6 A.M. Slowly he swings his legs over the edge of the bunk, combs his fingers through his thinning black hair, and stands up.

Matteo checks the compass, corrects the course a degree, looks up at the clock, and without a word moves away from the helm and descends the ladder into the forecastle.

Santo checks the compass, holds the course, slows the engine to three-quarter speed, and reaches behind him, first turning on the Loran, then the CB set. It begins to crackle. He switches to channel 3. No one is talking. He switches to channel 11. Just more crackling. He turns it down and goes over to the depthfinder by the port window and flicks it on. It begins to hum and the tiny needle begins to sweep down across the face of the white graph paper, leaving a small, black mark at the 40-fathom line . . . and another . . . and another, until a solid line appears. Santo pushes the helm to port, checks the Loran, checks the depthfinder. The black line is rising. It now shows 39 fathoms. Santo holds that course.

Below, in the forecastle, Matteo sits on the edge of the second bunk, which is used to hold extra equipment— spools of twine, pieces of net, floats, weights, tape, needles. He is pulling on his heavy, knee-length, rubber boots. A cigarette droops from between his tightly pressed lips. His face, as ever, is expressionless. Over his boots he draws black oilskin pants, slowly sticking in first one leg, then the other, pulling up one pant leg until the boot shows, then the other. He stands up and slips an arm through a fastened suspender, hoists his shoulder until the strap fits snugly by his neck, then reaches down along the opposite pant leg for the second strap, which is loose. This he swings behind his back and over the other shoulder, and fastens to the brass button on the top of the apron part of the pants-apron unit. He shifts his shoulders back and forth until the oilskins feel comfortable. He sits down again and takes two thick rubber bands and slips these over the boots, over the bottoms of the pantlegs just above the ankles, and lets them snap into place. The rubber bands seal the pants to the boots and no water should be able to wash up between them and into the boots. In summer wet boots are just sloppy, in winter they can mean frozen feet.

But almost as important, the rubber bands tend to lighten the weight of the bulky oilskins. For much of the fisherman's day is spent bending over, kneeling or squatting, straightening up, reaching down, stepping over fish or through fish, and always correcting for the roll of the boat. And the knees are constantly rubbing on the oilskins, tugging them down, and the shoulders are constantly hoisting them back up, and after a day's work on deck the back is aching just from the battle with the oilskins. The rubber bands stop the drag of the oil skins, forcing them to bag at the knees, letting the legs move around unimpeded. It's a simple thing. It helps.

Matteo walks over to the bunk where Mike and Anthony are still asleep. Like his father, Anthony sleeps on his side, his knees tucked. Mike is still straight out on his back, the visor of his cap pointed up at the ceiling.

Matteo taps Mike on the knee, taps him again. Mike opens his eyes. Matteo nods at him. Mike stands up and reaches into the bow for his oilskins and boots, sits down on the opposite bunk, and pulls them on.

Matteo climbs the ladder from the forecastle, stands at the head of the gangway, looks at the Loran, turns around and stares out over the bow, then heads aft. Mike follows. They haul the cod end toward the stern and check the knot at its end, making certain it's tight, that the strain of the tow, the weight of the fish flowing into it will not break it loose. Matteo clears away a basket that has become slightly entangled in the net, then the two men stand side by side along the starboard rail and gaze over the nearly calm ocean. In the distance a pair of draggers are already on the tow.

Santo slows the engine and throws the gear into neutral. The wake spreads out behind and disappears. He comes out of the wheelhouse and joins the two men at the rail. They study the water below them. Then Matteo takes hold of the cod end and pushes it overboard. Mike and Santo step back over the net and, in unison, pick it up and stuff it over the side. For a moment the net floats, then the water seeps through the narrow orange mesh and it sinks beside the boat. The three men return and watch to see whether it will drift under the boat or away from it. When there is a wind blowing or something of a sea, the boat will be carried away from the net, for the set is always made on the windward side. But in a calm they have to depend on the tide and it is uncertain at this point whether the tide has turned yet. The net drifts away.

Mike walks to the foreward gallows, Matteo to the after gallows, both on the starboard side. The gallows are heavy, U-framed iron stanchions with a block or bollard hung from the center. Through the block runs a wire or cable, one end of which is coiled on the winch by the wheelhouse door; the other end is attached to the doors which hang from the gallows. The doors are large slabs of oak framed with heavy steel. There are two of them, each connected to one side of the mouth of the net. When they are dropped into the water, they carry the net to the bottom. Once there, they act like foils on an airplane. As they are towed through the water, they are pushed out by the pressure of the water rushing past them. As they push outward, one to the left, one to the right, they pull the wings of the net with them and the wings in turn open the mouth of the net. The net at that point resembles a funnel with a stopped end. The entire operation is known as an Otter trawl. No one knows why.

The doors are carried between the gallows and the rail, and have to be lifted up by the winch and pushed out over the rail before being dropped into the water. Santo starts the winch. First he hauls up the forward door. With one hand Mike clenches the brace which stabilizes the gallows, holding himself out of the way of the swinging door which, on smaller draggers like the *Maureen,* weighs 500 to 600 pounds (on larger draggers they weigh over 1,000 pounds; they can crush a man very quickly—and have), and, as Santo releases the wire, Mike shoves the door away from the boat. It swings out and back and whacks on the side of the boat. Santo and Matteo repeat the process for the after door.

For the last time Santo checks the net. He can see the cod end hanging about ten feet underwater off the starboard stern. He goes to the wheelhouse, heaves the helm slightly to starboard, throws the gear into forward, and gives the engine full throttle. The net rises to the top of the water and stretches out in an elongated V.

Santo returns to the winch and carefully pulls in on the two cables, giving Mike and Matteo enough slack to free the hooks which hold the doors to the gallows. Then he releases the winch drum brakes . . . slowly . . . slowly. The doors start toward the water. The engine roar builds, the boat shakes. When the doors have just about touched the surface he lets the brakes go completely. The doors catch in the water and dive toward the bottom. The net disappears after them. The wires rush off the drums, lashing through the block, fathom after fathom stringing out and down behind the racing boat. Every twenty-five fathoms a piece of white tape appears on the salt-rusted wire and dashes into the water. At 125 fathoms Santo moves into the wheelhouse, slows the engine to quarter speed, comes back to the winch, and begins to apply the brakes. The wires cease to whip. Gradually they come to a halt. Santo returns to the wheelhouse and heaves the helm to port, bringing the stern against the two wires which are now in parallel along the side of the boat. He stops the boat and goes aft to help Mike and Matteo heave up on the forward wire and place it in a hook on the after gallows. Now the two cables cannot stray.

Santo goes back to the winch and loosens the forward drum brake, letting the wire out until its fathom mark is in line with the mark on the after wire. Then he tightens the brakes, returns to the wheelhouse, and gives the boat some forward speed—not much, just enough to keep headway.

He sets the hands on a cardboard tide clock to 8:15, the hour when the nets must be hauled back. On a piece of paper he writes his Loran bearing. He checks his depthfinder, sees he is still holding the 39 line, reaches for a length of line fixed to the starboard wall and slips the loop of the free end over a spoke on the helm, then stands back and relaxes.

Meanwhile, Matteo has appeared at the foot of the ladder with three more mugs of coffee and a large white paper bag. He sets the three mugs on the floor of the wheel-house. Mike, who is leaning against the port window, picks them up, gives one to Santo, puts one on the shelf, takes the last for himself. Matteo comes up with the bag, sets it on the floor, reaches in, and pulls out an unopened package of sweetened Italian milk cookies. He puts these on the shelf, opens the package, takes three, and then, with the cookies and his coffee, sits down on the bunk and begins to sip. Santo and Mike take cookies, dip them in the coffee, and take a bite.

In the half-hour it has taken to put on the oilskins and set the net out, not one word has been spoken.

# 3

## On the Tow
## and Hauling Back

The boats are on the tow. Off the Isle of Shoals Salvi has angrily set his nets outside the *St. John II* and is slowly moving off to the northeast. Spava has found a spot about three miles east of Halibut Point and, after having his wires snarled by a strong crosstide, has finally set a course to the southard. Tommy is just off Thacher Island in a small "hole" he knows, and is steaming east-by-south. Olly is on his favorite line off Long Beach and is heading east-by-north. Busty has set to the eastward of Eastern Point and is making his way south-by-southwest toward Baker's Island. And Santo is an hour directly southeast of the breakwater and is holding a southerly course for the moment.

The morning is clear. The visibility is nearly unlimited, and from each of the boats other draggers can be seen, some just specks on the horizon, others in sharp outline. Some are in pairs. There's a group off the near edge of Jeffreys Ledge. There are boats towing alone.

They seem aimless the way they meander across the ocean surface, some going this way, some that, others going this way, then that, then back again. There is nothing aimless about it. They are towing a "line"—a definite path across the ocean bottom a certain number of fathoms down.

Sometimes the line is straight, sometimes it bends like a horseshoe, sometimes in an S. Sometimes it is interrupted by a steep slope upward or a sharp decline, and then the boats have to turn around and return the same line. Or maybe they know the slope is only a hump and they can skirt it and come back on the line.

It's the same as the farmer plowing his fields. He doesn't plow on hillsides or down banks because he knows the crop he is planting won't grow well there, or that he may damage his equipment. The fisherman knows that certain fish like certain depths and certain kinds of bottom. The farmer knows enough to plow around trees and ledge and swampy areas. The fisherman has to cope with these, too.* For the ocean bottom is like the farmer's field, and both men know their ground intimately. The only difference is, the fisherman's field is usually over 100 feet below him. He's never seen it and hopes he never will.

But he knows what's down there because he's learned. He's learned from his father, he's learned from other fishermen, but mostly he's learned the hard way, by snagging on a rock or towing into a wreck and ripping up his nets and having to go in and lose the day mending. A good fisherman doesn't forget. When he rimwracks, or tears up badly, the first thing he does is find "marks." If, like Tommy, Busty, or Salvi, he is working within sight of shore, he locates a house, a tower, a water tank, things that will not vanish over the years, and he marks these down with the depth he was towing.

Some of the men, like Busty, keep their notes on small

---

* Off the edge of the Continental Shelf there are forests of what the fishermen call "trees," large, pulpy growths with trunks and branches that foul and often tear up the nets

sheets of memo paper, stack them in bunches, and wedge them for safekeeping behind electrical wires stapled to the wheelhouse walls. Others, like Santo, who fishes most of the time out of sight of shore and must locate hazards with Loran bearings, buoys, and depths, mark them on charts. Many of the offshore draggers who fish 50 to 200 miles from land and tow for miles at a stretch, moving from one fishing ground to another over two-week periods, keep such information in notebooks. It is said that an offshore captain's notebook is worth at least $200,000 a year, not only to its owner but to any other captain who might somehow come across it.

But a fisherman who must continually refer to his notes or to his charts is no fisherman. Once you've fished a piece of bottom, you remember it. You know that when you're working the 42-fathom line off the Isle of Shoals and you're towing to the northeast, when the first of the three peaks in the distance begins to fall between the tower and the white hotel on the island there is a wreck in the way and you haul to starboard until the peak hides behind the tower, then you come back again. Or if you're fishing Long Beach, you know you can come back the 37-fathom line until the spindle on Milk Island reaches the southern light, then go west. Now you can go until the big green tank is on the southern tip of the island. Then you pull back to the eastward. There's hard bottom in there.

You learn it all because it is expensive to forget. A net that's on the deck is a net that's not fishing, and when a net's not fishing the boat is not making money. In fact, it's losing it.

And you learn not only for the Isle of Shoals, but for Thacher, Long Beach, HalfHour, all of Middle Bank, all of Jeffreys Ledge, and, if you're hungry like the greasers, you learn the grounds off Cape Cod and at least as far north as Bar Harbor, Maine. You learn all the "holes," all the plateaus, all the muddy bottom where the flounder bury themselves, all the rocky areas where the groundfish—the cod, haddock, hake, and pollock—feed. You learn where the wrecks are, not only to avoid them, but also to brush them and pick up groundfish which feel safe there and like to spawn in wrecks.

If you don't know the grounds, all of them, as well as a taxi driver knows a city, you starve. Once that might not have been as true. Years ago, all a fisherman had to know was generally where the fish should be and he could put his nets over, tow for an hour, haul back, and fill the deck with fish. The price on the market wasn't high then, but there was enough supply that the fishermen made a good week's pay. As the fishermen say today: "All the old men had to do was find their way out and find their way back and they had a trip. They were good fishermen, the old men, because they did what they did without any of the electronic gear we have. But none of them could fish today." Tommy puts it this way: "If my father were fishing now, I'd have to put him on deck."

Busty's father, Cigar Joe, was one of the old fishing captains out of Gloucester. For years he had his own boats. The first was a schooner. Cigar Joe fished the Grand Banks, and he fished as far south as the New Jersey coast and everything in between. He didn't make a fortune fishing, but he owned his own house, his own boat, his own cars, and he supported his family well and raised two sons to be good fishermen.

"My dad would probably still be trying to fish now, even if he is 75," Busty says, "but one day . . . you see, he and I were battling over who should be taking his boat out

. . . one day I said to him, 'Look, I'm going to take a tow
down the 39 line and you bring it back the same way.' I take
the tow and we haul back with about 1,000 pounds of fish.
He brings her back the same line and gets nothing, may be
a couple of boxes. He says it's because I took all the fish,
so I says, 'Let me do it again.' I take her back down the 39
line—and remember, this is the third time through the area
—and I get another 1,000 pounds. That was the last time
he came fishing. He went ashore right then. He knew. You
can't fish his way anymore."

(Cigar Joe still rises early in the morning, gets into his
sixteen-foot runabout with a five-horsepower outboard and
goes into the outer harbor and sets a few gill nets. Initially
he found he was so successful he began setting out more and
more. "It was supposed to be his relaxation and he was
making it a business," Busty says. "The old guy was going
to kill himself, so we took away his boat until he promised
to go easy. Now he makes about $20 a week fishing, we give
him a share from the boat, he's got his pension. He's happier
than a pig in shit.")

Compared to what used to be, there are no fish today.
The fishermen must scour the bottom for them, dig them
out of the holes. There is no longer such a thing as "trash"
—fish like redfish, haddock, hake. These are now staples of
the market. Shrimp and squid, once sold as bait if brought
in at all, are big business. Even the lugubrious monk fish
which seems to be all mouth has a tail which the fishermen
lop off and sell to a European market hungry for just about
anything that lives in the ocean. The only fish that may be
thrown away are those too small to be boxed and iced, and
there are some fishermen who shovel these into boxes and
sell them to the fish dealers for tuna chum.

And that is why the first tow of the day is the most

important, that's why Salvi was so furious at the *St. John II* for beating him to the Isle of Shoals and getting the inside line. For the first tow is known as the "Morning Glory tow." It's the one that catches the fish as they school down from their night in the midwater. The men say that what you get in the first tow you rarely match in the subsequent tows because the fish are scattered and won't school again. Once, towing through a school of fish was like running a hand through a pile of grain—they spilled back together again once the tow was past. Now, there are so few fish one tow doesn't leave enough to regroup, which explains why most of the boats fish alone or at most in pairs. Too many boats in the same area and one pass leaves nothing to come back to.

* * *

Spava Bertolino has a seat hinged to the inside wall of the wheelhouse. Other boats have seats, but Spava is one of the few fishermen who uses one. It would seem to make a certain amount of sense. After all, most of the men are at the helm at least ten straight hours every day. That's a long time. A man can get tired, even if he's done it all his life. There's only one problem. When Spava sits down, he can't see anything except the inside of the wheelhouse.

But, then, Spava is a little different from the other fishermen. He doesn't worry about things like landmarks. They say about Spava that while his knowledge of bottom is limited, his ignorance of landmarks is almost total. And the man has been fishing the waters for thirty years. And making a living.

He sits alone, a thick, black, half-smoked, often-lit, dead cigar clenched between his teeth, one leg crossed over the other, leaning back against the wheelhouse wall, a bemused expression on his face. Something is running around and around in his head, something that for the likes of him he can't get a handle on. It's as though he can almost hear Nutzie saying:

"Why youse girls always picking on Spava? What's the Spava ever done to youse? He's a nice man."

Spava agrees, he is a nice man, and he would love to know why all the fishermen treat him so badly. As far as he can remember, he has never done anyone wrong. In fact, he feels that he has gone out of his way to make their life easier. Wasn't it his idea to cut off monk fish tails that created the small market everyone else enjoys? And wasn't he the first to bring in shrimp and hand shell them and take them around to people, and aren't shrimp now big business in the city? Look how everyone is making money off his ideas and what credit does he get? Why no one even recognizes the ideas were his to begin with.

"I don't say nothing," says Spava. "I don't complain. I'm glad. Somebody's making money."

Spava cannot talk without inserting at least one "you won't believe it" and one "I don't complain," and then setting forth a list of complaints that are hard to believe.

He has been crushed by a full bag of fish that "came into the doghouse after me"; he has ripped the ligaments in his arm so that he couldn't lift it for months; he's had gallstones, ulcers, concussions, and high blood pressure. Before World War II he built a new boat and the government promptly requisitioned it for patrol duty and then tried to sell it back to him at twice the price they paid for it—and he was still trying to pay off the debt incurred building the boat in the first place. His *compare* Salvi Testeverde has twice tried to run him down while they were fishing together. You might expect that from other fishermen, but not your *compare*. Why, a *compare* is the closest friend you've got, outside your parents and St. Peter.

But the thing that makes Spava feel saddest is that Tommy and Busty will not talk to him on the CB set.

"It goes like this. I see Tommy. I tell him I got fish, he should come. So he tells Busty and Busty comes. So we are all fishing and I hear them talking. All day they're talking and they're right there. Right there! I hear them but they don't call me. They don't say, 'Spava, how many fish you got?' You don't believe it? I'm telling you.

"So I don't say nothing. I don't call them. I say, 'You call me first, I'll call you,' but they don't call. Then you know what happens? You won't believe it. We're all at the wharf and Nutzie comes over and says, 'What's the matter, Spava? You not talking to us? All day we fish with you and you don't say nothing.' Now, how do you like that?"

It's not altogether true the others do not talk to Spava. More often than not he hasn't got his CB on. This is strange because for most of the fishermen the CB is their only companion in the wheelhouse. They turn it on before they reach Ten Pound Island. All day long it crackles and spits and vies with the roar of the engine below. They rarely get off it. "Without it," says Tommy, "we'd go crazy. Of course, Spava's CB is a little different from the others." Even when it is on it is frequently off. There's a loose connection somewhere which the vibration of the boat breaks and the set goes dead. Spava has solved the problem. He goes over and hits it and on it comes again.

Spava glances up at the battered depthfinder on the back wall, squints at it for a second, then goes back to pondering. He has to squint at the depthfinder because the paper in it is so black with so many old lines that it takes time to distinguish which is the line he is supposed to be reading. The fact is, the paper doesn't fit that machine. Not only does it belong to another depthfinder (and therefore the depths on his machine do not coordinate with the lines on the paper), but the paper has already been used on the machine it was designed for. Spava can't remember whose machine it was. It might have been the *St. Bernadette*'s, but then it could have come from the *Santa Lucia.* It doesn't make any difference. It was being thrown out and that would have been a waste of paper. Spava is not known among the fleet as "Linsky" for nothing. Linsky is the local junk dealer.

"I hear the boys on the radio, they're talking about something they got to fix. I tell 'em, 'Don't buy that new, go up to Linsky's. Save yourself some money.' They never do. I don't know why."

Spava also doesn't know why the other fishermen refuse to embrace what he calls "the Spava tow." While everyone else tries to get in at least three tows a day and, if the fishing is good, a fourth, Spava sets out twice and tows back and forth across the bottom for hours. His net may be ripped up and there may be no fish in it at all or the cod end may be stuffed with dogfish which have no market value and only eat the smaller fish around them. Spava wouldn't know. And besides, long tows do nothing for the quality of the fish. Dragging may be the most economical method of bringing in fish in bulk, but when the fish are all jammed together in the cod end, all twisting and turning on one another and bouncing along the ocean bottom, the effect is the same as running them through a scaling machine. Once a fish, especially the softer fleshed fish like whiting, are in the net, their quality immediately begins to deteriorate. And since the inshore boats make their money on quality, not quantity, there is a reason for the shorter tows.

Spava argues that he can catch as many fish as the others by simply filling the net fuller, that it is a waste of his time to be constantly hauling back. It means more work for his crew, more strain on his boat. He doesn't understand why the others show no more appreciation for this innovation than they do for his Linsky advice.

But there is a reason. The other fishermen do not respect Spava. Spava has "no class." It is one thing to be idiosyncratic. Everybody knows that when Salvi is on fish, he doesn't talk on the CB. When he's not catching, he's talking all the time, always trying to find out who has fish and where they are. That's Salvi's way. They accept it because they know Salvi takes his fishing seriously, that when he is making money he shares it fairly with the crew and that the shares he keeps for the boat got to the boat and not into his pocket. Salvi may be a hard man to deal with, no one is going to say he is a hundred percent honest, but Salvi is a good fisherman. Tommy may hate fishing and he may play with his gear too much (and everyone knows that sometimes Tommy reads pornographic literature on the tow, especially if the first set wasn't much), but they recognize that within his limitations he is a good fisherman —and fair.

But everybody knows that Spava can't keep a crew because he doesn't pay them, that he takes his settlement at the end of the week and arbitrarily gives his crew $25, maybe $50, when deckhands on other boats catching no more than Spava are earning $200, $300 a week. The way Spava figures it, if you don't want to work for him, find another site, if you can. Usually they can't because Spava hires only nonfishermen, men with no experience and no family contacts with the waterfront. It's hard to find a site without contacts. It's even harder with no contacts and no experience. Spava knows that. And he understands that a man who has never fished before can't expect a full share of the week's earnings. And while he can always train someone to handle the mechanics of deck work, at any time he can prove that the man doesn't know how to mend twine, splice cable, repair the winch, or work on the engine. Spava sensibly keeps these things to himself so that the deckhand is never worth a full share.

Making money off the crew is not class. And then, when Spava refuses to put any money back into the boat except for an annual painting, so that the mast is permanently cocked, rain washes through the decking into the galley, the winch brake wheels sit on shafts which have corroded to the thickness of a pencil, half the nigger or gypsy head has cracked off and catches the lines being wound around it, the wood along the rails is rotting despite the layers of paint, and the auxiliary pump has to work all night because the boat leaks so much, well. . . . Maybe that's his business. All right. But when Spava steamed past Olly last year when Olly was about to go on the rocks and then later claimed he hadn't seen Olly, that was pushing toleration past forgiveness.

And that's why this spring, when Spava had engine problems and couldn't go out for three weeks, no one came around to help him. "How you doing?" they would ask, and Spava would shake his head and say, "I don't know. I can't find it," and everyone would say how too bad that was and walk away and go out fishing. And the weather was good, too, and the boats were making money. And Spava sat there and everyone knew what the matter was. It was a simple problem. Any good fisherman could have done the work in a couple of days. Finally they began to feel sorry for him. They wouldn't come right out and tell Spava what to do, but they dropped hints and after awhile Spava heard them.

And that's why they began to lie to Spava. Everytime he fished with them they would call him up and ask him how many fish he'd caught on his last tow. He'd tell them and they'd say that was too bad, they guessed they were just lucky but they'd gotten a couple more boxes than that. It made no difference how many they'd actually caught. Sometimes Spava had more, but they always added a box or two. And after a few days of this Spava began to worry. Never one to make many adjustments on his gear, still Spava worried that everyone was catching more than he was. No fisherman can take that pressure for long. So Spava began making adjustments. Still the men kept claiming more until Spava's gear wasn't fishing at all and he had to lay in for a few days and straighten it all out.

But the real fun came when a Boston television station did a special on the plight of the fishermen and wanted a "representative" dragger out of Gloucester for some footage on what fishing is really like. The producer came down to Fisherman's Wharf and asked the men for their advice. They gave it. They pointed to Spava Bertolino and his dismal dragger *Clinton* and said, "That is a real representative of the Gloucester fishing fleet." Spava made the best week's pay he'd seen in years, the producer got his footage, and the men thought it was the funniest thing they'd seen —Spava Bertolino representing the fishing industry.

\* \* \*

# ON THE TOW AND HAULING BACK

GLOUCESTER DRAGGER *St. Providenza* TO GLOUCESTER
DRAGGER *Cigar Joe II:*

*Busty. Busty. Come in, Busty.*

*Ha-low, Tommy. I hear you. Yeah. Where are you,
Tommy?*

*Thacher's, Busty. That little hole I told you about. I
don't know what's here. We'll see. We'll see. . . . Busty, was
that Hillary I saw coming in? Looked like his boat.*

*Yeah, Tommy. A hard-looking craft, ain't she? Hard-
looking craft. I had a boat looked like that I'd bury it. You
know?*

*Yeah, yeah, Busty, I know what you're talking about.
Give him a chance. She won't be around for long.*

*That's right, Tommy. How many's he had? What—
three now? The silly bastard. I don't know. Someday maybe
he'll find one he can keep floating.*

*Ha, ha. Yeah. Ha, ha. Maybe . . . Busty, I've been
having this idea. You know we got to make some money and
I got this idea maybe we should have a revue . . . like down
at the Dugout. You see, I got it figured this way. We'll get
Nutzie to dance and we'll get Sammy of the* St. Bernadette
*to sit in the corner and sing "Old Black Joe" like he does,
and right in the middle of the thing we'll have Hillary come
and streak through, and while everybody's trying to figure
what's happening, you and I'll come round with hats and
we'll make enough to stay in the week. Wha'd'ya think?*

*That's beautiful, Tommy. I like that about Hillary, but
you got me worried. You know, Hillary's got that big stomach of his and I bet when he streaks nobody'll be able to
see if he's got what he's s'posed to have. And, Jesus, if he
don't have that, nobody'll give anything to see him. You got
a problem, Tommy.*

*No. I got that figured. After he runs through, we hold a pool and everybody puts money in to see if he's got it, and when we got enough, we bring Hillary back and he shows us. They'll love it. I know Sammy'll sing "Old Black Joe" again.*

*Well, you work on it, Tommy. I think you got something. Anything's got to be better than what we're doing out here.*

*Yeah, I'll work on it, Busty. I'll work on it. . . . When you hauling back?*

*Soon now. Soon as I make the mark here I'm going to haul to the eastward a few minutes, then I'll see what I got.*

*Yeah, well, I'm about the same. I got another fifteen minutes, then we'll see. . . . There's a bunch of boats off to the eastward. I seen two of them haul back a few minutes ago. Can't see what they got. There's too many a them out there. I'm staying here. Maybe they'll shy the fish right into me. Who knows? Something's got to happen. This is starvation.*

*Ain't it? I'll tell you, there's not enough out here to get the frying pan out for.*

*I know, I know. Well, I see Olly's hauling back now. I'll call him, see what he's got. Let me know what you get. Maybe I'll take a tow down that way, I get nothing. I don't know.*

*O.K., Tommy. Be back later.*

*Yeah. Finest kind, Busty. Later.*

* * *

Olly has no fingernails left. He bites them constantly. He stands at the helm of the *Sea Buddy*, staring alternately at the depthfinder, then out the starboard window at the

shore, sighting on a high, narrow, white house, waiting for
it to move over and sit on a long, narrow, white house so
that together they will form an inverted T. When that
happens, he has to turn off the line and miss a wreck.

He looks down through the window and checks whether
the bilge pump is working. There's no water coming out the
hose, so he reaches behind him and pulls up a string to start
the pump, wrapping it a half-dozen times around a small
knob on the panel covering the fuses. He checks the hose
again. Water is spurting out.

He reaches down by the compass and picks up a half-
empty pack of cigarettes. They are lying beside an unopened pack. There are a dozen matchbooks scattered
around with the cigarettes, none of them full. He taps the
opened pack until the filter comes out. He grabs it, sticks
it in his mouth, snatches up a matchbook, twists a match
off, and hurriedly lights the cigarette, checks his
depthfinder, takes the line off the helm, heaves the helm to
port, and loops the line back over a spoke.

He looks at his right hand and sticks his index fingernail
between his teeth and nibbles away at the corner. He looks
at the nail again and nibbles some more. He squashes the
cigarette out on the lid of an empty soda can, steps back
through the door of the wheelhouse to the deck, and flicks
the three-quarters-unsmoked butt off the port side. A seagull dives down on it, buzzes it, and settles into the water
and watches the boat pass.

For a moment Olly stands on the deck, one hand gripping the doorjamb. He looks off the stern at the boats
fishing past Thacher Island. He glances at the wires stretching aft off the starboard. They are spread out in an elongated V, each leaving a tiny wake as they cut like fins
through the water. They are pulling straight, not jumping

the way they would going over rocky bottom. They're not flip-flopped so they're not snarled. They're pulling right. That's good.

The *Sea Buddy* is barely moving. Olly is out for flounder and flounder bury themselves in the mud, so that the net has to dig them out as it passes over the bottom. If the net is moving too fast, it will slide over the flounder and pick up whiting instead. The whiting like the mud, too, but tend to rest on top of the bottom so that the net can cut underneath and scoop them in. The whiting tow is only slightly faster than the flounder tow, for, despite their long, slim, strong bodies, the whiting swim slowly.

Cod and haddock are faster and require greater speed on the tow, and the pollock is the greyhound of the groundfish and can easily swim back out the mouth of the oncoming net. To get pollock the boat has to be towing wide-open, something the fishermen rarely do. For excellent as pollock is to eat, there is no market for it. The meat has a brownish color and people are too set in their ways. Fish is white. If it is brown, there has to be something wrong with it. So the men don't waste the time or fuel, and the pollock, the only victim of apartheid in the ocean, lives to thrive another day.

There are two reasons Olly goes after flounder. First, the price. At $35 a hundredweight, with four or five boxes of gray sole he can make as much in a day as the other boats will with fifteen or twenty boxes of whiting. And there are also fewer fish brought up in a flounder tow, which makes it easier to clear the deck. Which leads to the second reason. Olly is one of the few fishermen who work alone.

"I'm captain, crew, wife, and slave to this boat," Olly says. "I'm it. It's mine. I don't have to worry about anyone. I fish when I want, where I want, and as long as I want."

They say about Olly: "He has a strong back and just few enough brains to be a good fisherman. His only trouble is, he worries too much." They also say Olly is one of the few fishermen who loves fishing.

Olly did have a deckhand earlier in the year, a kid named Ryan. Ryan came from Billerica, a factory town an hour inland. He brought a loud mouth and his brother's Social Security card with him, and it wasn't long before Olly discovered Ryan was making $200 a week with him and then going up to the Division of Employment Security and taking another $100 a week "social" under his brother's name. That might have been all right, but Ryan began calling Olly's New York dealer to double-check on the amount and price of the fish Olly was sending down. That was too much.

"I was giving the kid a full share. He couldn't mend. He couldn't splice. He couldn't do shit except cull fish and bitch. Then he starts going behind my back. Fuck him. I gave him a week's pay and told him to get lost. Who needs it? I was doing most of the work myself anyway. I might as well keep the money."

And why not? Last year Olly took home $17,000 after taxes. The boat made over $20,000. Five years ago he was making almost as much as a deckhand on an offshore dragger, but staying at sea two weeks at a time, at home two or three days, and back to sea for another two weeks. It didn't make sense. Olly was "hungry," but not so much that he was willing to give up three-quarters of his life, 250 to 300 days a year, isolated with five other men on the deck of an eighty-foot boat surrounded twenty-four hours a day by nothing but ocean and fog and heaving seas, knee-deep in fish most of the time, getting three hours of sleep here, two hours there. For what? So he could make enough money so the old lady would have a nice house and a nice car and the kids could have nice clothes and nice food, all of it a little bit nicer than he could afford, none of it something he could really enjoy because he wasn't around enough to enjoy it.

There was only one thing to do and he had to do it before he got too old, too married to that life. He was a fisherman. Fishing was the only thing he knew. He'd been worth a full share since he was fifteen and he'd fished summers for years before that. But now he'd become his own fisherman, he'd buy his own boat and he'd get his father to join him, and they'd fish as a family like so many of the other boats.

But right away Olly had problems. Unlike Busty, who couldn't get his father off the boat, Olly couldn't get his father on. Both older men were lifelong fishermen: the sea was the only thing they knew, but they knew it and lived with it in converse ways. Cigar Joe had always been a captain and Gaspar Palazola had never been, nor wanted to be, anything other than a deckhand on an offshore dragger.

As a deckhand Gaspar was Number One, one of the last of a breed of fishermen for whom the deck of a dragger is home, and a house and family are things to visit every two or three weeks. Physically, Gaspar and his eldest son are of the same mold—tall, iron-hard, straightbacked men. Gaspar's black hair is turning gray, but like Olly's it is short and curly and all there. Both men like to laugh, but only Olly lets himself. Gaspar just smiles like a man who has spent his life taking commands from men who rarely know as much as he does.

And there is very little Gaspar does not know about the deck of a dragger. There is nothing the sea can show him that he hasn't weathered countless times before. Not only can he endure it year after year, he loves it. It satisfies him.

Others around him have grown tired, their backs have weakened, they've become sick and left. Others have become captains on other draggers. Some have bought their own boats. But for Gaspar there is only one life, that of the deckhand. That's the only place he wants to be, and no matter how Olly urged him, cajoled him, painted this picture and that picture of the good life they could have together on their own boat, how they'd be their own bosses, how they'd fish where and how they wanted and they'd be home every night and they'd make enough money they could stay in ever so often and go down to Mitch's and shoot pool and drink with the rest of the boys, Gaspar resisted. He did waver. He said he might. He even became enthusiastic when Olly found a small boat in New Jersey they could get for a good price. But when it came to putting down money, to taking on debts and responsibilities he'd never had to face before—and, in truth, had lived his life avoiding—Gaspar ran back to the forecastle, to the bunk with the crumpled blankets, to the wet oilskins and the week after week away from home. At sixty-five years of age Gaspar Palazola was too old a dog.

Olly bought the *Sea Buddy* anyway. She was over forty years old and under forty feet long, big enough to take rough weather, yet small enough to fish alone. None of the local banks would back him for the downpayment. Public Finance would, however, at an exorbitant rate. That was four years ago. The boat was paid off in full in two years. Last year she turned a profit. This year she will realize that profit and half again as much.

But the engine is showing its age and there's something wrong with the rudder assembly, and fuel has doubled and ice is up and twine is unreasonable, and there is no sense thinking about insurance it is so prohibitive. And the boat needs a radar and that's $6,000 at least. A lot of gray sole. Maybe he can get by another year without one, and maybe the engine will hold out another couple of years, and maybe he can fix the rudder himself and not have to put the boat on the ways because, Jesus, is that expensive! And if the summer weather extends into fall and if the winter is as quiet as it was last year and if the market stays strong on gray sole and if he doesn't get hurt and if . . .

Olly goes back into the wheelhouse, checks the depthfinder, looks out the window, and sees the two houses closing in on each other, glances at the hose, sees only a trickle pulsing out of it. He turns off the pump, takes the line from the helm, heaves it hard to port, stands back from the the helm and watches aft as the two wires come together, cross over one another, then spread apart, checks the two houses once more, hauls the helm back to starboard, lashes it steady again, and reaches for another cigarette.

* * *

There is something in a seagull that knows intuitively when a boat is about to haul back its nets. All morning there has been scarcely any sight of the gulls. Occasionally one will swoop down and perch on the transom and look around the deck for a scrap that hasn't been washed overboard, but mostly it will just stand there surveying the sea, its flat, glassy, yellow and black eyes darting, never resting, and then, for no apparent reason, it will lean off the transom, seem about to fall into the water, and, with a thrust from its spindly legs, will arch into the air and disappear.

And sometimes the boat will pass a gull squatting in the water, riding up and down on the wake, or in the distance there will be two or three gulls languidly floating low over the surface. One will dive, there will be a splash, and it will scoot away shaking its head and find a place away from the others to eat. And once in awhile a Mother Cary's chicken will mingle. Much smaller, dark brown with touches of white, dashing low and fast, skimming the water, it races away like a fighter plane.

But if a dozen gulls are seen on a two- or three-hour tow, it is rare, and it means only that the herring have not dived to the bottom where they spend the day before surfacing at night, or there is a school of tuna chasing them. Sometimes a tuna will break water and the men will search frantically around the forecastle for a hook and line to throw overboard. By the time they find it, get it unraveled and baited, the tuna is gone. They say the hell with it and put the hook and line back where they won't be able to find it when they want it again.

Then suddenly the gulls begin to appear around the boat. There may be only a handful, but the flock grows. They seem to know that the two hours, three hours, however long the tow may be, is up.

And almost invariably the engine slows and the boat comes to a stop.

* * *

Santo turns from the helm and sits down on the bunk. At rest against the starboard wall by his feet are his black rubber boots. He puts them on. He does not wear oilskins. He doesn't need them. Clearing the deck is not his job. He goes to the head of the ladder and calls Anthony, who is sitting on the edge of the bunk, rubbing his eyes and pulling up his hip boots. "Hauling back," Santo says quietly. Anthony nods and comes up the ladder, reaches into the white paper bag for a cookie, takes a large bite, and follows his father on deck.

Matteo is putting the last checkerboard in place, fitting it into slots built into the port side and the hatch amidships, forming a pen about six feet by eight feet and a foot high on the deck. The pen is set on the port because the boats tow off the starboard. If the pen for the fish were placed on the same side as the tow, there would be no room to put the net if it had to be repaired or when, after the last tow, it had to be stored.

Mike has gone aft and has popped the forward wire out of the hook on the after gallows, and, once the wire is free, Santo takes the brake off the winch drums which begin to turn, slowly at first, then a little faster, and the wires rise silver-gray wet from the water, through the gallows block, and wind up on the drums.

Santo concentrates on the incoming wires. They do not wrap evenly on the drums but want to follow on top of the coil before and slip off to either side. Mike and Matteo pick up long, steel rods which they jam into holes drilled in a plate fixed to the deck before the winch. They push and pull the wires, forcing them across the drums. It's important. When the next set is made, the wires must run free. They cannot pinch or bind, or they'll wrack the winch and stretch and weaken themselves.

Unlike setting out, when the speed of the boat against the drag of the doors and the net pulls the wires off the winch and the only worry is letting the wires run out too fast, the labor of hauling back falls solely on the winch. There are 175 fathoms or 1,050 feet of wire out, at the end of which are two 500-pound doors, and behind the doors a 100-foot net with at least 1,000 pounds of fish. And they all have to be hauled straight up through more than 100 feet of water.

The wires are taut. At odd times they slip on the drum and snap back. The boat shudders, and a shiver runs their length, springing pellets of water into the air. The engine groans. It seems to be on the verge of giving up, then regains its strength. The boat is heeled over. As the net slides along the bottom until it lies directly under the boat and the wires angle in toward each other amidships and the net begins to rise off the bottom, the boat heels over even further. No one is relaxed. Everyone is tense. This is the time when wires snap and snake across the deck, when shackles break, when welds give. When these things happen someone gets hurt. And there is nothing anyone can do about it. It happens too fast.

At last the doors break water. Santo stops the winch. Mike goes forward, Matteo aft. Each stands poised just inside the gallows, the hook for the door in one hand, the other hand firmly gripping the brace, their feet spread wide apart against a sudden roll of the boat. First Santo brings in the forward door, slowly easing off the brake, gradually raising the door until the V.D. hook holding the wire to the door hits the block. With a quick twist on the brake wheel he stops the wire and holds it fast until Mike hooks the door to the gallows. Santo eases back on the brake; the door slides backward, catches on the gallows, hook and hangs there. Mike slips the V.D. hook from the wire, heaves the freed wire over the after side of the door, and stands back. Santo and Matteo repeat the process.

Santo sets the brakes hard and goes into the wheel-house, puts the boat in gear, heaves the helm to starboard, and gives the boat full speed. The net, which has sunk alongside the boat, spreads out along the wake. Santo stears a wide arc, driving the fish that remain in the broad belly of the net into the narrow cod end. The entire net rides along the the surface, the orange-red mesh of the belly and the green mesh of the cod end frothing the blue sea white. The gulls flock down on top of the seething net, pecking and pulling at the tails and heads of the smaller fish that have been caught half through the mesh. Two gulls fight for the same head and turn viciously on each other, while a third gull sweeps in unseen and yanks the head clear and escapes.

When the net is again to the windward, Santo stops the boat, throws it out of gear, and steps back to the winch.* He takes the brakes off and rolls in the remaining few fathoms of wire which, free of the doors, run directly from the tips of the net's wings through the gallows block to the drum. When the wings reach the block, Santo disengages the drums, leaving the nigger or gyspy head turning.

Once the wings are raised, all four men go to the rail and pull them inside. With the wings come the headline and footrope, which they drop with their weights and floats, snug along the length of the rail. Then they bend over the rail and, digging their fingers into the mesh, in unison heave the slack belly up in folds, shaking it like a sheet, tumbling the few fish that have escaped the cod end down along the net.

When there is no more slack, Santo returns to the winch, unties the gilson, or the block and tackle, and holds

---

* When there is a sea, the weight of the net acts as an anchor holding the boat from drifting too far off course. The boat, though heavier, rides higher in the water and the wind and waves drift it to leeward enough to keep the net from running under it.

The principle is the same for setting out, only then the net, being empty of fish, is lighter than the boat and tends to follow the boat, which is being pushed sideways by the seas.

the line while Anthony takes the hook to Mike, who has squeezed the net together like a furled sail. Matteo hands Mike a short strap about three feet long with loops on either end. Mike wraps the strap around the net, pulling it tight, bringing the two loops together and hooking them on the gilson.

Santo takes a double turn on the niggerhead, puts pressure on the line, and draws the net up. When it is about ten feet overhead, he slackens off the gilson, the net falls to the deck, and Matteo and Mike jump to the rail and hold the net from sliding back overboard. The backward slide is stopped. Mike takes another squeeze, again a strap is wrapped, again the net is raised and lowered, and now the entire belly is on deck in a pile. Only the cod end and the fish remain outside.

A double-thick strap is now wound around the top of the cod end, an extra turn is made on the niggerhead, and the bag comes up, higher, higher. It clears the rail. Water pours out of of the bag in a torrent. The mesh is stuffed through with the gaping heads of small whiting suffocating from the crushing weight of a ton of fish bearing against them and nothing but deadly air to breathe. The bag swings like a pendulum across the boat. The boom above moves after it. The bag hangs for a second over the pen, then comes back to starboard. Matteo and Mike let it finish its swing, then step behind it, dig their shoulders into it, and propel the bag back across to the pen. The boom comes over the pen; the bag stays, suspended two feet above the deck.

Both men reach for the line knotted in binding loops at the bottom of the bag. There are two ends. One of them is attached to the first loop of the knot. It's impossible to see which one it is without getting down on hands and knees.

They pull one end. Nothing gives. They grab for the other end, pull it. Nothing. Mike gets down on his knees and looks under the bag, wary of the weight hanging just over his head. He separates the two ends, follows each to the first loop, gets up, holds the right end. Matteo and Anthony grab it with him. They yank . . . yank again. Something gives. They grab the second end. It comes. Now the first, now the second . . . until the bottom of the bag begins to spread open.

The pressure of the fish drives the hole wider. Fish slide across the deck like bits of sand pouring from a bag. Santo raises the net up and the fish wash out in a jumbled mass and fill the four corners of the pen. Some spill over the checkerboards. The men stand there nearly up to their knees in wriggling fish. They kick their way free, dragging the cod end with them. Santo lowers it to the deck. Anthony unhooks the strap, heaves it into the stern by the shrimp boxes, and passes the gilson to his father, who hooks it on the winch and makes the line fast to a cleat on the mast.

Santo looks the fish over. He says nothing. Mike reties the knot on the cod end while Matteo examines the belly and wings for tears. There aren't any. The two men haul the cod end off the pile of fish, across the deck, and heave it overboard. Anthony joins them as they follow the cod end with the belly, then the wings. The net spreads out on the water and slowly sinks. Santo throws the engine into forward while Anthony releases the brake drum. The wires pay out. The doors are hooked to the wires, are unhooked from the gallows, drop into the water. The boat surges forward. The engine roars, everything vibrates. The doors and net disappear below. The wires lash off the drums, fathom after fathom. The boat slows. Stops. The engine quiets. The wires are evened off and hooked parallel. The second tow of the day begins.

It is 8:30 A.M.

# 4

---

# *Culling the Fish and Clearing the Deck*

*T*ommy is disgusted. He stands looking at the pen of floundering fish and mumbles, "Cigarettes. Nothing but goddamned cigarettes. What the hell are we doing out here, you can't get nothing but cigarettes?"

He's got to call Busty. He's got to talk to somebody. What a stinking business. Three hours on the tow and nothing but a bunch of "cigarettes." Whatever happened to the big whiting? Might as well wash the whole bunch of them overboard. What's in there—three boxes, four boxes? The first tow and three boxes of whiting, not even half a box of flounder. Doesn't even pay the fuel bill. Yeah, he's got to talk to someone about this.

But the CB is blaring as he climbs back into the wheelhouse. The goddamned pogie boats are taking up the air and there's no way to shut the bastards up:

*Easy, Joe. Easy, Joe. Easy now. Steady, steady, steady. To port, Joe. More, more. Too much. Come back, Joe, come back. Hold it, hold it. They're coming at you now. Go easy. Easy. To starboard, Joe. Easy . . . EASY. That's good. Hold it . . .*

Tommy has a grin on his face. He listens as Vito Calomo directs Joe LoGrasso toward the school of pogies, or menhaden, swimming just under the surface in Salem Harbor, an hour to the southward. Vito is in a small plane circling over the seine boat, spotting the pogies. Joe is in the seine boat below. He can't see the pogies and is steering blind. Vito says it's a good school, maybe 50,000 pounds, maybe 80,000 pounds, he can't tell, but there's a bunch of them down there.

"Watch this. I bet he loses them," Tommy yells through the open window at his brother Nutzie, who is squatting among the fish, trying to find some whiting big enough to toss into the wire basket by his side. The deck and rails are crowded with gulls honking and biting each other and occasionally streaking down on the mess of fish and stealing one away from Nutzie's or his son Billy's hand.

"Get outa here. Get outa here," Nutzie screams at them. "We don't need none a youse girls around here. Haaa!" And there is a wild flapping of wings and the gulls leap off the rail and tread air until Nutzie turns his back, then they perch once more on the rail and start honking again.

"That cocksucker. You think he's going to put Joe on fish when he's got his father out there, too? You better know he isn't," Tommy says. "The kid couldn't go home if he did that. What a racket!"

There's no doubt, Vito has a conflict. He spots for two boats, the *Agatha & Patricia* and the *Ida & Joseph*. The trouble is, the *Ida & Joseph* belongs to his father and its crew is either family or *compares*. There's no family on board the *Agatha & Patricia*. Spotting for her is a straight business deal. So what's Vito to do? Business is business, but family is family, and in this case family is also big business.

There's a lot of money in pogies and the way the boats have been sweeping them in this year the men are making $200 to $300 a day. The *Ida & Joseph* is used to that kind of money. If she doesn't have 200,000 pounds of pogies on deck ready to be reduced to fish meal by the end of the day, someone is going to hear about it. And that someone is Vito. Still, the *Agatha & Patricia* pays him well.

*They're coming at you now, Joe. Get ready. Get ready. Hold it. Not too fast. Get ready . . . O.K. Now, Joe. Let the net go. Let it go. Faster, Joe. Faster. You got 'em. Faster. Close it up, Joe. Close it up. Close it, close it, close it . . . oh, Jesus! Joe, they're gone. They slipped right through. You gotta close faster. I don't know where they went. Maybe you got something, I can't see. Maybe there's something in there. I don't know what happened.*

"That's right, Joe," says Tommy. He's laughing like a bastard. "He don't know what happened. . . . Now let's see what he can do for his dad."

"Haaa! Outa here. Outa here," Nutzie bellows. Billy stands up and looks at him. There's a pained expression of pride on his face for this man with the squashed-down, grimey hat and the mouth full of gums and a few decaying brown teeth, kneeling in the middle of the potpourri of fish and water, screaming at seagulls laughing all around him.

"Wha'd'ya want with my goil? Wha'd'ya do with my goil?" Nutzie begins to sing. Badly. "Wha'd'ya think a my g . . ."

"How do ya turn this guy off?" Billy asks, looking back at Tommy, who is leaning out the window.

"Listen to the baby, how he talks to his papa," says Nutzie. After all, that is the voice that allegedly wowed them in California years ago. Nutzie says so.

71

"You're scaring the fish," Billy says, unrepentant.

"The baby needs a backhand, maybe," Nutzie suggests. They both go back to culling the fish.

*I see 'em, Joe. Come ahead. Come ahead. Slow . . .*

"Get off the damned radio," Tommy yells. "Why do those guys have to use this channel? They know it's the one we use. Ten channels and they have to use this one."

*Easy now. Port. Port. Good. Ho . . .*

"Go faster. Go slow. Go home." Tommy starts giving orders. "Don't listen to him, Joe. He's going to put you on a rock."

Tommy gives up. He hooks the microphone back on the radio, checks his marks, takes the line off the helm, heaves her to port a few degrees, and lashes the helm again. He walks across the wheelhouse and sits down on the end of the bunk, reaches down into a large cardboard box at his feet, and takes out a paperback with the front cover ripped off. There are a dozen more paperbacks in the box, all with their covers ripped off. Three or four are dog-eared and the spines are broken from having been laid flat open on the bunk and sat on.

Tommy adjusts his horn-rimmed glasses, leans back against the wall, and begins to read about the widow who discovers her son is growing up. The son discovers Mommy but finds Sis isn't bad either, and the dog gets his licks in, too. If nothing goes wrong, Tommy can finish it off before hauling back again.

"Cigarettes. Shit." Tommy opens to the first page.

\* \* \*

Salvi was right. There should have been fish on the Isle of Shoals and there were. He hunches over the helm and stares at the overflowing pen and figures fifteen boxes of whiting at least. That makes him angry again. If there were fifteen boxes on the outside line, what did the *St. John II* get inside—twenty? And now the guy is an hour into the second tow and the grounds are crowding up fast. There's the *Serafina II,* but she's staying outside. Let her stay outside, that's not going to bother Salvi's tow. And there's the *Little Flower,* and the *Santa Lucia*'s right alongside. What is this, a convention? The hell with it. Get fifteen boxes this tow, maybe ten the next, so maybe there's only seven or eight the last tow. Thirty-three boxes, that's a good day's work. Everybody will make some money.

Salvi calms down. He's getting too old to get excited. He watches his son Joey and old Tommy Frontiero working on deck and Salvi feels relaxed. At last he's got a crew he can work with. It's a relief to have that eldest son of his, Johnny, off the boat. Jesus, but didn't they fight something! You couldn't tell the kid nothing, knew everything, everything about what was wrong, that is. Big like his father, but the temper. It was all Salvi could do to match it. The two of them would start in before the boat had even left the wharf in the morning. "Where you gonna fish?" "Isle of Shoals." "The Shoals is for shit, they're catching good in the Bay." "Fuck the Bay, the Shoals." And they'd be standing there face to face. You could fry an egg if you could get it between them. And then they'd start shoving and hitting, and there wasn't anyone around who wanted to try to stop it. Four o'clock in the goddamned morning! And they'd go at it that way for the rest of the day until Salvi's nerves were so worn he'd be falling asleep at the helm, and Tommy and

Joey had reached the point they didn't want to fish anymore for fear one of those two was going to kill the other.

But it was family. How do you tell your own kid to pack his clothes? You don't. You keep on fishing . . . and fighting . . . until finally Johnny quit and found a site on the *Agatha & Patricia.* Now Salvi can fish like other fishermen— quietly.

And the difference! That Joey. A good boy . . . educated. He's got a degree in electronics from trade school. He wouldn't be fishing but there is no work around and the kid just got married and he needs the money. He works hard, doesn't say much, does what he's supposed to . . . a good boy.

And Tommy. The finest kind. Fishing for years. Knows everything there is to know about the deck. Quiet, unassuming, shows up every morning and goes right home every night. Pays his rent on time. (Salvi knows. Tommy lives in one of his apartments.) Tommy's only problem is, he gets seasick. Most fishermen get seasick once in a while, particularly after being ashore for a time while the boat is laid up. But most of them get used to the sea after a day and it doesn't bother them. Not Tommy. For years he's tried to go offshore, but everytime the weather blows up he starts feeding the fish. That's why he has stayed with the inshore boats. When the sea is too bad, the boats come in or don't go out at all. It's a good life for someone like Tommy, whose only real vice is occasionally playing the dogs at Wonderland—$1 on the seven and eight without variation.

* * *

To a fisherman a fish is nothing more than a fish, the way a row of corn or potatoes is just a row of corn or potatoes to the farmer, something they harvest and sell and someone buys and someone else eats, and what do they care as long as they get their money.

Money. That's the thing. The cod may be sacred in the state of Massachusetts, but it's sacred because for 150 years it has been worth steady money. The haddock is a beautiful fish, strong and silver-gray with a thin, black line running along its side. On either side of its neck are two dark spots. The fishermen call these the thumbprints of St. Peter, the patron saint of fishermen. It is understood that St. Peter placed the haddock in the ocean for the fishermen to catch and make money. The men feel no compassion for the poor flounder who is forced to live its adult life swimming on its side with both eyes on the other side staring upward and its mouth twisted between the sides in a snarl. They gaff it in the head, flip it into a wire basket, and say to themselves, "35¢ a pound."

Santo looks at the overflowing pen and quickly calculates $150. Not good, not bad. He knows he has to make at least $450 a day to break even. There is the crew to pay and that is three full shares counting himself, a half a share for Anthony, four shares for the boat. There are two tons of ice in the hold at $14 a ton and 100 gallons of fuel at 39¢ a gallon. There's a $12,000 bill for rebuilding the deck, another $2,000 for winch repairs. Insurance on the men is $600 a man and for the boat another $4,000. It adds up, and Santo does not fish to break even. He has begun to buy some real estate. He has a nice house that was just painted. His wife has her own car. He doesn't live high, but when he wants to take a vacation he doesn't want to think about where he can't go. If he wants to visit relatives in Sicily, he wants to take his entire family, plan for three weeks and stay a month, the way he did two years ago. Last year he took the family to California.

But most important for Santo is the boat. The *Maureen* must remain in perfect shape. "I have to be able to get to the fish wherever they are and, if the weather blows up, I want to be able to get home. I don't ever want to worry about it. I mean, how do you fish if you have to worry?" But not to have to worry takes money, and that means fishing hard and long. And the harder and longer you fish, the more money it takes, so you fish even harder and longer and hope that someday you will come out the other end with more money than you need, so you can relax. That's the greaser point of view.

Santo can't understand Tommy and Salvi and Spava, and he is disappointed in Busty. "They're lazy," he says. "All they do is fish the same old grounds, over and over, and they catch fewer and fewer fish. They don't make any money. They say the fishing is bad, and you know what? They have to go as far to get nothing as I do to catch fish. You don't see any of those guys out here.

"Busty used to fish with me and we did good. I showed him places and he made money. But then he got in with those other guys and now what's he making—$10,000 a year. I don't see how he lives on that. Busty's a guy who likes a good time. His family must be starving."

Santo does know why Tommy and the others rarely come out to Middle Bank. The boats are too old and there is usually a sea running on Middle Bank. And even when it's calm, the tides are strong and the engines have to labor to hold the tow. So the boats might make money for awhile, but sooner or later the seams would begin to part and the engine would start to fail and all the money they had made would vanish in repair bills.

And besides, Santo is almost right. There is a kind of laziness. It's not that they don't fish hard, it's that they are not hungry. They are making money, not much, but enough. They prefer to relax.

Santo is not ready to relax. Someday, not now. He wouldn't know where to begin. Twenty-five years ago he arrived in Gloucester from Sicily. He was eighteen years old. Like most of the Sicilian immigrants in Gloucester, Santo came from a fishing village. Fishing was all he knew. So he went offshore dragging. He lasted a year.

"I couldn't do it. I said to myself, 'For what do I come to America—to spend my whole life at sea? I don't see my family. I don't see nothing.' Crazy!"

He was nineteen and he bought a small, thirty-foot dragger and began fishing in the Bay. Like Olly twenty years later, he fished alone. But, unlike Olly, he didn't have anyone to teach him the grounds, to let him follow on the tow. Those were big-money days and the old captains were vicious.

"I'd wait for one of the old captains to go by, then I'd come right behind. When they set out, I'd set out. They didn't like it. So pretty soon I'm finding I'm getting hung up all the time, I'm getting rimwracked good and having to come back in and mend. I couldn't afford but one net in those days."

What was happening was that the old captains would set their nets overboard but would only let out a few fathoms of wire, knowing full well they were going over a piece of bad bottom. Their nets would be suspended in midwater, safely above the rocks, while Santo's net would be hard on the bottom.

Santo learned a basic lesson from those old captains: don't trust anyone in the fishing business; even your best friend will lie if he's on fish.

Once he realized he would get no help from anyone he began teaching himself. He learned all the bottom up and down the coast. He fished seven days a week, bad weather or good, winter and summer. "I was young, then, and I guess I was a tough fellow. I didn't care. I wasn't married. Then I got married, but I didn't have no children right away, so I had lots of time. There were times I'd wait until the weather was real bad, when I knew no one was going out, then I'd fish in tight along the shore inside the limit. I knew the Coast Guard wasn't going to come after me. I had to fish like that—my boat was too small, I couldn't go outside. And sometimes I'd fish at night along the shore when nobody'd think of looking for me. I didn't care. So sometimes I'd get caught. I've paid a lot of money in fines. I've made a lot of money, too."

He has, but none of it goes to the Coast Guard anymore. Santo doesn't have to fish inside. He knows where the fish are outside and he has the boat and crew to go get them. It has taken a long time and a lot of hunger, but now, at the age of forty-three, Santo has almost everything he wants. There is just one more thing. He wants Anthony to fish with him. He dreams of the day he and Anthony will be the crew of the *Maureen* and of the day he turns the *Maureen* over to his son. Captain Anthony Militello. Santo likes that.

That is why Santo bought a small dragger, one that can be fished by two men, and didn't follow his brother-in-law Johnny Cusumano to the big boats. Cusumano's *Acme* is the newest boat in the fleet: only three years old, a big, strong, hard-working boat that makes big money. But she needs five men on deck and she has to fish long hours because the expenses on a boat sixty-five feet long are enormous. And, like Santo, Cusumano does not fish to break even. He is very hungry.

The *Maureen* is not a new boat. She was built in 1946 in Newport, Rhode Island. She was falling apart. She leaked. Her engine hadn't been overhauled in years. She was the right size.

Today she looks newer than Cusumano's *Acme.* The wheelhouse has been raised and widened. The entire midsection of the deck has been cut out and replaced with heavy metal sheets. The engine has been rebuilt. Every year she is scraped down and painted bright red with dark-green trim, the colors of the Italian flag which Santo flies from the mast along with the American flag.

The wheelhouse interior is white with dark-red trim. So is the forecastle. There are rugs in both. It's an extra touch. There are no rugs on the *Cigar Joe II* or the *Linda B,* the *St. Providenza,* the *Clinton,* or the *Sea Buddy.* Their wheelhouses were painted once sometime ago, and a couple of times before that. It's easy to tell. Count the flaking layers.

The *Maureen* today is a proud boat. Anthony stands in the forecastle and says,"I did this and, you see, no red on the white. It was hard," then laughs an embarrassed laugh. Anthony is only fifteen years old. On his way into the forecastle Anthony sees a smudge on one of the dials set into the board by the helm. He stops and cleans it off. No one told him to; it was just dirty. Santo picks up a coffee mug, sees that it has left a ring. While he is taking a sip, he wipes away the ring. It's a reflex.

But what pleases Santo most about the boat is that nothing short of an engine failure can force him to stop fishing until he wants to. In the wheelhouse he has two depthfinders, two radars, two Lorans, two CB sets. "If something goes wrong, why should I have to wait until it is fixed. My radar stops, I take it ashore. I leave it. The next day I go fishing. You see that boat there? Already it goes in. Rimwrack. He loses the whole day. He has no other net on board. I rimwrack and in twenty minutes I have a new net tied on and I'm fishing again.

"I don't know. Some people, they don't think ahead. They don't want to spend the money. They say they'll get by. How can they? You have to spend the money, then you make the money. At least that's what I think."

*  *  *

Something happens when the fish hit the deck after the first tow. For three hours the boat has been plowing back and forth across the ocean surface. The men have lain on their bunks in the forecastle or sat in the wheelhouse, sleeping or staring, not saying very much—just waiting. Some, like Busty and Sammy, drink one cup of coffee after another. Spava has a fried-egg sandwich. Tommy hangs on the CB. Olly smokes cigarettes and bites his fingernails.

And 150 feet below, out of sight, the net is working its way along the bottom, scraping everything in its path into its gaping mouth. Or at least it should be gaping. But is it? Are the doors hauling right? Are there enough weights on the footrope to keep the net down, or is it riding too high and the fish slipping away underneath? Has it slid over a jagged boulder so now there's a tear down the belly and the fish are swimming through? Are there fish down there to slide under or swim through? And if there are fish, what are they and how many?

How do you know? There's no way to tell. Ever so

often, the depthfinder shows black specks above the bottom, but are those from fish coming down from midwater or are they just echoes from the electronic signal bouncing off the bottom? There is a temptation to haul back and see, like bringing up the hook and line to find out whether anything has been nibbling at the bait. But you don't bring up a 100-foot net that way. You leave it down there and you tow the line because you know that once there were fish along that line. Three days ago you got a good bag of fish out here, yesterday you got a bunch of dogfish. Are the doggies still down there or have they moved elsewhere? Who knows? But you have to keep going, you have to make a living, you have to take the chance. So there's no fish, you move somewhere else. You can't let it bother you—there's always tomorrow. Patience is the fisherman's second greatest virtue. Eternal optimism is his bread and butter.

Then the cod end swings aboard and the fish spill out on deck and for a moment the men look down at the mess in front of them, a wriggling, flapping, seething confusion of tails and fins and hundreds of blankly staring eyes, black bodies, red, green, gray, silver bodies, gaping mouths fighting frantically for breath, the tails of small fish dangling from the mouths of larger fish. A rusted beer can. An old pot. Some pieces of rope. Strings of seaweed. Clumps of mud.

The worrying is over. That—whatever it is—is what you've got. The net is back overboard, the next tow is underway. You've got to get the stuff off the deck. You can't stand around and curse. There's no shaking hands and telling the captain what a fine tow he just made. All the captain has done is his job; now the crew has theirs.

And it's not a nice job. There are 2,000 pounds of fish lying there in a heap. An hour before they had been swimming along the bottom looking for food, living together in the vicious peace that exists in the ocean, and suddenly they had found themselves mashed together in the tight cell of the net, turned over and over on themselves until they were upside down, sideways, wedged in every conceivable angle, unlikely pairs in a mortal congregation from which no escape is possible. And in this jumble they had been hauled up from their natural homes, some of them already expired from the crush around them, others still fighting, squirming, trying to drive their way to freedom through the small open squares of the mesh containing them, their pointed heads squeezed through, their bodies caught inside. And the net rising like an elevator carrying them into a height they could not bear, gasping for air, their bladders swelled and burst into their mouths like balloons.

The men set to the job immediately. Mike goes to the stern and pulls out a stack of three wire baskets, separates them, and throws them onto the pile of fish. Anthony and Matteo seat themselves on the checkerboards, worm their feet under the fish until their boots are flat on the deck, then reach down and start throwing the fish into the baskets.

There are two baskets for the whiting and another for the mud hake or ling. The whiting is a long, finely tapered, black-over-gray fish with a firm body which belies the fragility of the meat. It bruises easily and begins to deteriorate upon entering the net. The fishermen heave them into the baskets. They slide over the rim and stretch out along the bottom, piling up like kindling wood. Because whiting are narrow and strong they are easily picked up with one hand gripped around their backs, and can be thrown with accuracy. The ling, on the other hand, is a soft fish. It feels like a balloon filled with water and it is coated with slime, so it frequently slides through the hand unless the men squeeze their thumb and fingers around the neck and catch on the gills.

Mike wades into the fish, digging his feet through the mass until he finds a firm footing. Then he bends over and starts culling some of the cod which have slid into the corners. He inserts his middle finger deep into the gills, plucks the cod out of the corner, and flips it onto the deck in the stern.

Anthony reaches for the deck hose which is hanging off the port rail and begins to hose down the fish, washing the mud off them. The pen fills with water and the fish start to float off the pile. Matteo clears away a free space in the corner between the checkerboard and the port gunwale where a small, wood gate or door hangs shut. The cleared space fills with water and small whiting, American eels, carbuncles, periwinkles, and mud. He slides the gate up a few inches and the water rushes out, carrying the trash with it. It spills overboard and spreads out on the water. The gulls hovering just off the boat sweep down in a flurry and pick the water clean.

Mike kicks his foot around in the pile, clearing fish away from a large monk fish which is buried up to its tail. The monk fish is something of a monstrosity. It has a huge mouth which is practically as large open as its body is long. It has a top and bottom row of sharp teeth which are angled inward, and it swims along the bottom with its mouth wide open, much as the net does, and gorges on whatever gets in its way. Many a fisherman has ruined a good pair of rubber boots by stepping into a monk fish's mouth.

The monk fish does have a long tail which, when cooked properly, tastes like veal. The tail is so slimey that it cannot be grabbed, and unlike most fish, the monk has no gills. This makes it difficult to pick up. Mike kicks around until he is certain he has the top of the "monkey's" head. He takes his middle finger and pokes it through the fish's eye, wriggling the finger around until he can bend a knuckle over the eye socket bone. He hoists the fish up, grabs the tail, turns the fish mouth down, and shakes it until all the whiting and herring lodged inside slide to the deck. The mouth emptied, Mike heaves the monk fish to the stern with the cod and haddock. It lands with a squishy thump and slides on its belly and short, splayed fins that look curiously like hands, until it ends nose up against a shrimp box.

As the fish wash down off the pile, the tail of a dogfish emerges, wagging slowly back and forth. The dogfish is a small shark. It is gray with a long, wiry, streamlined body sometimes over two feet long, a slightly flattened nose, and a mouth with tiny, razor-sharp teeth. The dogfish is good for nothing. Because there are so many of them, especially in the summer when they come inshore after whiting and mackerel, the fishermen have tried to sell them. But a single dogfish will dull a sharp knife and the time required to dress them for what little eatable meat they carry is not worth the trouble. It is simpler to throw them overboard.

But tossing a dogfish overboard can be hazardous, not because of the teeth, but rather because of the two sharp bones camouflaged in front of the two dorsal fins. The bones are not only needle sharp, but they are painfully poisonous, so much so that fishermen have had to go to the hospital after being stabbed by one. So Anthony is cautious as he grabs the wagging tail with both hands. He tugs it free of the pile, shuffles to the port rail, and swings the dogfish down hard, smashing its head. He swings it a second time, then drops it overboard. It lies there for a moment on its side, then rolls over, belly up. The gulls fly down on it and fly away. Gulls are not fond of working for their meals.

Gradually the pile of fish diminishes. Three baskets of whiting sit full to the rim. There are two more filled with ling, and the stern deck is strewn with cod, haddock, large hake, and monk fish. There are some gray sole and yellow-tail flounder in one of the shrimp boxes.

Matteo and Anthony are down on their knees, reaching into the pile, grabbing whiting and tossing them, squeezing ling and tossing them, flipping cod and haddock to the stern deck, opening the gate and washing the trash out, shooing away the braver gulls perched on the rail. Once in awhile they come across a squid and throw it toward the door of the wheelhouse. Sometimes there's a small, flat butterfish or a young haddock. They throw these toward the squid.

Santo leaves the wheel, lashes it with the becket, and, taking out a fish knife, cleans the squid, dresses down the small haddock, picks up the butterfish, and carries them all to the hot muffler just aft of the wheelhouse in front of the winch. He arranges them around the exhaust pipe on the flat, round head of the muffler which is stained black-brown from the fish that have been cooked there before. With the tip of the knife he nudges the fish around, making certain they cook evenly. Then he gets a pail and starts culling out some of the larger shrimp that came up in the tow.

The *Maureen* normally fishes for shrimp, but, owing to the boycott the boats have set up against the local shrimp processors, Santo has designed the tow to get only a few shrimp. Santo knows Middle Bank. He knew that if he fished a line along the foot of the bank, he'd get mostly shrimp; if he towed along the top he'd get groundfish. So he tried to hold the middle of the slope where he would get a little of both.

Unlike the crew, Santo has not bothered to put on the denim work gloves and instead rakes through the shrimp with his bare fingers, picking out the two-inchers. He scoops up a handful and pours them into a pail, scoops up another handful and lets out a muffled yelp, drops the shrimp, and begins shaking his index finger. Sticking into it is a bright-orange quill. For, besides its hard carapace, the shrimp comes armed with a number of very sharp quills that stick from its head. The quills can pierce a set of rubber gloves and often will break off once they've entered the skin. Santo takes out a small penknife, opens it, and begins to dig out the point of the quill. Finished, he shakes his hand again, then reaches back into the shrimp for another handful. These he puts on the muffler with the fish which are already beginning to sizzle. An admixture of deisel exhaust and frying fish wafts across the deck.

There are no more baskets. They are all full. Mike and Matteo each take an edge of the hatch cover and lift it to one side. Mike leans across the open hatch, grabs the two sides firmly, and drops his lanky body into the hold. He finds a long iron rod that looks like a furnace stoke and begins to chip at the pile of crushed ice in the stern. He breaks off a number of chunks and hits these until they split into small pieces. He takes one of a number of boxes stacked three high along the sides, and flips it over so that it sits open and empty. He picks up a shovel lying beside the ice and puts a layer of ice in the bottom of the box, turns around, and looks up.

Matteo takes hold of the nearest wire basket, hoists it waist high, shuffles through the fish, humps the basket over the open hatch, and lowers it into Mike's waiting hands. The full basket weighs close to a hundred pounds. In one motion Mike takes the basket and, turning quickly, lets it come to rest on the edge of the box. He upends it and the whiting slide onto the bed of ice. With one hand he spreads the fish out evenly; with the other he slings the empty basket back up on deck. Anthony catches it and drops it in the middle of the unculled fish.

One after the other the baskets are lowered, emptied into boxes, ice is shoveled on top of the filled boxes, and a lid is tacked in place. The lid is slightly bowed as though there were either too many fish or too much ice. By the end of the day the ice will have melted enough, the fish will have compacted, and the boxes will come out of the hold four-square.

Mike hauls himself out of the hold, slides the hatch cover back in place, and joins Matteo and Anthony as they cull out the remaining fish. So far it has taken about an hour to reduce the jumble of fish to baskets of whiting and ling. There are enough flounder for another full basket, and the stern deck is littered with groundfish and monkeys.

Matteo and Mike take fish knives from behind the hatch and sharpen them on an old whetstone with rounded edges and a belly. Each grabs a cod, pinching its head at the eye sockets, getting a firm grip, and, turning the fish belly forward, slit it across the gills. The motion is quick and straight, and the fish breaks backward as though its neck had been snapped. The men then drive the tip of the blade into its stomach just below the gills, and with another single motion rip the stomach almost to the tail. They flip the dressed cod back into the pen. Anthony takes it by the head, inserts his thumb at the head of the rip, and pushes the thumb down the underside of the backbone. Like a snowplow the thumb scrapes the entrails from the stomach so that they hang down from the fish toward the deck, dangling alongside the tail. With an abrupt tearing motion, he yanks the entrails free and tosses them overboard and drops the fish behind him.

It is an assembly-line process: slit, rip, plow, and tear out, drop it, next . . . and on and on. The pile of dressed fish grows. The hake takes longer because the heads have to be severed. The monk fish is laid on the rail and the tail cut through. But there is a thick bone down the middle, so the first cut is to the bone, then the bone is broken on the edge of the rail and pushed down until it snaps. A slash severs the bone and a third cut lops off the tail. The body is shoved overboard; the tail is tossed back with the other dressed fish.

Anthony washes down the pen, shooting a jet into the corners, reaming out small whiting or herring that have become wedged there. As the baskets come back on deck, he hoses these down. They are covered with a thin layer of slime. Scales stick to them. There is slime and scales everywhere, and already the warming morning sun is working and the fetid smell of decaying fish is rising from the deck.

Finally he turns the hose on himself. First he sprays off his boots. Next he takes off his work gloves, sticks them into the flow from the hose, wets them thoroughly, and wrings them out. He takes the gloves and scrubs his arms. Scales stick to the light hair, are glued to the skin. He gives the gloves a final dousing and wringing, washes down his oil-skins, and hands the hose to Matteo.

The men stand there. The deck is glistening in the sun. The baskets are stacked once more in the stern. The men look around. Mike sees a line that isn't coiled. He coils it and hangs it on the after gallows. Matteo sees a shrimp that was missed in the scrubbing down. He twists the head off and sticks the entire raw body, shell and all, into his mouth. He chews on it and chews, tips his head down and spits out the shell, tips his head back and swallows the meat.

Santo goes over to the muffler, pokes at the cooking fish with his knife, turns to the men and nods, takes a few hot shrimp for himself, and returns to the wheelhouse. Each of the men walks over to the muffler, looks the fish fry over, takes out his own knife, and scrapes a perfectly flaked fish onto the palm of his hand. They sit down on the hatch cover. Matteo stretches his short legs toward the starboard rail. Mike crosses one leg over the other and, bending his neck, brings his mouth down to his cupped hand and takes a bite of the hot fish. Anthony goes below to the icebox and gets a can of grape soda, then comes back on deck and leans against the wheelhouse doorframe, and stares at the gulls astern still fighting over the remaining scraps.

Santo leans out the door and yells quietly above the roar of the engine, "How was it?" It is not clear whether he means the cooked fish or the tow.

Mike looks up. Dribbles of fish hang out the corners of his mouth. "Good," he says. "Good," and goes back to eating his fish.

# 5

## Coming In, Taking Out, Going Home

GLOUCESTER DRAGGER *St. Bernadette* TO GLOUCESTER
DRAGGER *St. Providenza:*

*Hello, Tommy . . . Tommy, come in. Jesus!*

*Sammy. I didn't see you, Sammy. Where are you?*

*Off Jeffery's, Tommy. Jesus, God Almighty, I nearly got
run into by a whale just now. I thought the thing was going
to come right on board.*

*'S that right, Sammy. I've heard that happening. I
never seen it.*

*Thought it was going to foul with the tow. Fucking
thing scared the shit outa me.*

*I can understand that, Sammy . . . Sammy, you catching
good?*

*Fifteen boxes . . . twenty. I don't know for sure. First
tow was good. Didn't get nothing the second. I'll probably
go in after this one. What you got?*

*Cigarettes both tows. I don't know, Sammy. I think we
better put these boats up for sale, take what we can get, and
buy a farm.*

*I know, Tommy, but who's going to buy 'em? Nobody
wants a fishing boat, for Christ's sake! What we got to do*

91

*is hold an auction 'n sell 'em off piece by piece.*

*That's right. Like a barn sale. Nobody wants the whole thing, but Jesus! if they won't buy the pieces. I don't know. It's crazy.*

GLOUCESTER DRAGGER *Cigar Joe II* TO GLOUCESTER DRAGGER *St. Bernadette:*

*Sammy. Sammy. Come in . . .*

*Hey, Busty. Yeah, Busty . . .*

*Sammy, that's rotten of you with that whale. All it wanted to do was mate with your boat.*

*I tell you, Busty, I wasn't laughing. You know what that thing coulda done. Jesus! I'da never gotten it outa the gear.*

*I know. Back a couple or three years we had something like that. We got a blackfish\* caught in the tow, you know. Didn't know it but all the sudden there's these blackfish swimming right behind the boat. We hauled back and there was that fish in the net. We got it on deck, didn't know what to do with it. We guessed it musta been dead, so we put the gilson on it and put it back over the side. Funniest thing. Those blacks came right up to the boat and just sat there whining. I mean, they were crying like babies. When we got their friend back in the water, they just started swimming around in circles around it, crying and nudging it with their noses like they were trying to bring it back. I mean, we felt like crying too. It was a real sad thing.*

*I can see that, Busty. I can see that. . . . How is it where you are?*

---

\* A blackfish is a small whale a little bit larger than a porpoise. Like the porpoise, they swim in schools.

# COMING IN, GOING HOME

*We got a day's trip, Sammy. We'll be hauling back in about half an hour. . . . Tommy?*

GLOUCESTER DRAGGER *Cigar Joe II* TO GLOUCESTER DRAGGER *St. Providenza:*

*I figure another half-hour here, Busty, then we're going back to the barn. These goddamned doors still aren't fishing right. They're still rusting on the back of the shoe. Gotta do something with them. I don't know what.*

*I don't know, Tommy. I got a pair you can try if you want. They're too big for me, maybe you got the power. Try 'em if you want. . . . Well, I gotta make a turn up here, starting into the back country. . . . See you back at the wharf.*

*O.K., Busty, see you back there, probably an hour, an hour and a half. When I get inside the towers, I'll haul back and head in.*

*That's good, Tommy. Bring Olly in with you. He's buying.*

*Good, Busty, I'll grab him on the way in. O.K., Busty . . .*

\* \* \*

The boats come in the way they go out—when they want to. On board the *Clinton,* Spava has engaged his semiautomatic stearing system and has left the wheelhouse and is seated on a box filled with trash fish for tuna chum and is dressing and filleting small ling to take home for supper. The gulls are hanging all around him, some hovering no more than a couple of feet over his head, their necks craned toward the fillets Spava is skinning.

93

Spava knows they're there. It's a game. Can he get the skin off and the fillet into the basket at his feet before the gull snatches it out of his hand? There's a sudden flurry of wings, the gull drops down, the tip of its wing touches Spava's hat. Spava whisks the fillet toward the basket, the gull flies off with a small chunk in its beak.

Olly has no automatic pilot. He stands on deck, one hand on the rail, his feet spread out like two legs of a tripod. He is bending forward toward the wash of flounder on deck. In his right hand he holds a gaff, a short stick with a pointed spike driven through the tip. He swings it down, gaffs a gray sole in the head, and flips it behind him into a wire basket. He gaffs a yellow-tail, flips it. He gaffs and flips and gaffs and flips, and once in awhile looks up and off to shore, then along the gunwale over the bow toward the bell buoy off Eastern Point. The boat is pulling to starboard. Olly drops the gaff, climbs over the fish to the wheelhouse, and corrects the course. He climbs back and continues gaffing and flipping, setting up an empty basket and flipping more gray sole into it.

Behind him a gull has found a small dab. Like all flounder, the dab is flat with a tough, slippery skin. The gull is not certain what to do with it. It is not like other fish. The gull cannot just pick it up with his beak and break it in half and swallow it. He picks it up by the tail and tries swinging it. He tries beating it against the transom. The dab won't break. He slips his beak under it and takes it in the middle, but the dab is too wide and flat and his beak is too weak and short. He can't make a dent. He throws it down on the deck, stares at it, then begins to peck at its head. No good. He starts pecking across the middle like a stonecutter splitting a block of granite. He pecks furiously, then grabs the tail again and whacks the fish on the deck.

The dab is breaking. He pecks some more, whacks again. The dab is bending. He grips the tail and pulls it up toward the head. The dab slides up the deck and is stopped by a box. The tail folds neatly to the head. The gull opens his beak wide, clamps the doubled-up dab as deeply as he can, and chomps a few times. The flesh is now torn. He sets it down, rips out some meat, swallows, rips out some more until the center of the dab is gone. He folds it one more time, gets a good grip on it, and flies off.

For the first time in twelve hours Salvi has given up the wheel and is letting his son Joey bring the *Linda B* down the Bay toward the Annisquam River. If Salvi has it figured right, the tide should be turning just as the boat reaches the lighthouse. That means she should be opposite Merchant's Island and coming down on the Route 128 bridge before too much water has run out of the channel and the *Linda B* might ground out. It's taking a chance, but if he can make it, he'll save at least an hour. Otherwise he'd have to go around by Thacher's and it would be five o'clock before he got in, six o'clock before he got the fish taken out at Fisherman's Wharf, and six-thirty before he was tied up and on the way home.

Salvi is tired. All day long he has been standing at the wheel. He hasn't allowed himself to rest, to relax, always watching the marks, remembering the wrecks, what kind of bottom lies ahead. He has been on deck only three times, to handle the winch setting out and hauling back, then it's been back to the wheelhouse, watching, remembering. He leans his elbows on the sill of the open window and rubs his eyes. It's been a long day for a fifty-seven-year-old man.

"Watch out for that pleasure boat," Salvi warns Joey.

"I see it," Joey says. "He'll turn."

A small yacht is coming out of the mouth of the river and is holding to the outside of the channel which is bordered on that side by a succession of sand spits hidden by the high tide.

"Don't trust the bastards," Salvi says. "Look at that . . . he don't even see us. Where's the guy at the wheel? For Christ's sake, there's nobody stearing the thing. What the . . . ?"

Salvi reaches over Joey's head and pulls down on the cord for the foghorn. There's a blast and suddenly two men appear out of the pleasure boat's cabin. The boat veers sharply out of the way. One of the men waves to the *Linda B.*

"Wha'd I tell ya! Someday I'm going to sink one of those bastards. They think 'cause they've got all that money we gotta get outa their way. They'd put us on the sand and wonder what the Christ happened. Jesus!"

Salvi slows the *Linda B* down to quarter speed and takes the wheel back from Joey, who goes out on deck and up to the bow and sits down next to Tommy. Tommy is cleaning squid on an overturned box, cutting out the eye and the small stinger hidden below its tenticles, slitting it down the middle and scraping out the innards, then throwing the flattened squid into a bucket. He'll take them home, wrap them in bread crumbs, slice them up, and lay them in a skillet of hot butter. A little treat for the old lady.

A small sailboat tacks across the channel. It should clear the *Linda B.* There's a boy and a girl in it, and both have a can of beer in their hands. Salvi holds his course. There's Merchant's Island just off the starboard bow. The sailboat tacks back.

"Where is that guy?" Salvi yells. "I can't see him." He

throws the engine out of gear, then jams it in reverse. The *Linda B* slows, momentum carrying her forward.

Joey leaps to the bow and holds up his hand. Salvi races the engine in reverse. The *Linda B* stops. Out from underneath the bow appears the sailboat. The boy and girl are sitting upright. The beer cans are gone. Salvi puts the gears into forward again and goes to the open door and stands there glaring.

The *Linda B* passes Merchant's Island. That's the halfway mark. Now the tide is running out with the boat. She steams under the Route 128 bridge, makes the wide turn to port, and heads toward the Boston & Maine railroad drawbridge where the river takes a hard right. The bridge is narrow, the turn is totally blind, and, with the tide at the stern, Salvi no longer has complete control of the boat. There is no chance of stopping dead if he should meet another boat coming under the bridge.

He gives two long tugs at the foghorn. He listens. There's no answer. He swings wide, increases the engine speed, and heaves the wheel hard to starboard.

Tommy and Joey are both at watch on the bow. They can just see under the bridge. Salvi can't. Joey lifts his arm and motions forward. The bridge attendant comes out of his small shack along the tracks far above the river. He could signal the channel is clear, but that is not his job. Raising and lowering the bridge is what he gets paid for, and he does no more.

Once past the bridge, Salvi cuts back to a quarter speed and lets the tide carry him downstream toward the Blynman Bridge at the cut that opens into the outer harbor. It comes in sight. The bridge is down. There are two pleasure boats ahead of him idling. Salvi slows to a near stop and begins to fret. The channel is too narrow along this stretch.

There is no way he can turn around if the bridge doesn't open. It stays down. He tugs at the cord. A blast. Cars continue to drive across the bridge. He tugs again and throws the engine in reverse. The boat slows to the speed of the tide. Salvi can now read the names on the sterns of the boats ahead.

The cars stop. A line forms. There's a ding-a-dinging ringing sound, and the bridge begins slowly to break in half. The pleasure boats do not wait until the bridge is all the way up. They move ahead and through the bridge, their antennae poking between the two rising halves.

Salvi waits, then eases the engine forward. The channel through the bridge is narrow and the water is rushing. It pulls the boat from side to side. Speed is needed to hold a straight course. The *Linda B* is heading into the cut when a speedboat starts into the other side.

"Get the fuck outa the way," Salvi screams. His face turns a deep red. The speed boat can't hear him, but it sees him. It stops dead, its overpowered outboards race as they are jammed in reverse, raising the stern out of water and forcing the engines to eat air. It backs off quickly, turns abruptly, and vanishes into the outer harbor.

"I don't believe it. Did you see that guy? I'da killed him," Salvi fumes as he moves into the outer harbor and turns for the Fort and the channel into the inner harbor. "I'da killed him . . . I shoulda."

* * *

"How much you got?"

Santo hasn't even made fast to the John Wright & Sons wharf and already they're yelling at him.

"How much you got?"

The way they crowd to the edge of the wharf and inspect the deck of the *Maureen* below, they resemble the gulls that have been hovering around the boat for the past twelve hours. There is a temptation to go "Haaa!" and see if they wouldn't all retreat to the safety of the old, low-slung, gray warehouse at the end of the wharf.

Twelve hours ago when these guys were still sound asleep, Santo and his crew were halfway out to Middle Bank. Eight hours ago while Santo was hauling back for the first time, these guys were just rolling out of bed and thinking about getting themselves off to work. And now here they are yelling, "How much you got?" and the only damn they're giving is that it's not too much because they want to go home and get some food and go out on the night.

Santo pretends he doesn't hear them. He steps out of the wheelhouse and leans over the rail and watches Anthony and Matteo make the lines fast. Then he goes back in and turns off the engine. For the first time all day the boat is silent. The silence is filled by the din of the city at work.

Santo grabs hold of the oily, weed-scummy, barnacled wooden ladder and climbs up onto the wharf. He looks around. A tall, older man in a clean, gray workshirt and khaki pants with three ballpoint pens and a small notebook in his breast pocket comes over and stands next to him. They shake hands. The man's hands are clean and soft, but big and heavy as though at one time they, too, might have been greasy and oily and had shrimp quills dug out of them.

"Wha'd'ya got, Santo?" the man asks.

"Must be twenty boxes whiting, probably ten large cod, same a scrod, some gray sole, maybe a box of tails, and two boxes of shrimp. I don't know exactly."

Santo knows exactly, but he's not saying. He wants to know from them what he has. Santo hasn't been in the fishing business all his life for nothing. Thirty years ago the old fishermen led him on the rocks and he learned: don't trust other fishermen. But fishermen belong on the right hand of God compared with fish dealers. You don't choose a dealer by his honesty, but by his degree of dishonesty. The fishermen assume all dealers are thieves; it's just which will rob them the least—or is most willing to share in the thievery.

"Look out," a heavy, pock-faced man yells. The boom on the wharf winch swings low over Santo's head. He ducks as it sweeps out over the now open hatch. Matteo, impervious as always to the yelling and chatter and banter, the running back and forth along the wharf of the two jitterbugs, or forklifts, hauling empty boxes here, full boxes there, grabs the rope dangling from the tip of the boom and pulls out enough slack to hand the end into the hold to Mike.

The end of the rope has two broad loops attached. Mike fixes each loop over the lips on either end of the top of the box. Matteo takes a strain on the rope; the loops grip under the lips. He raises his left hand and the old man at the wharf winch takes a double bight with his end of the rope on the niggerhead. The box rises out of the hold. Matteo holds it back so it does not bang on the hatch. It clears and he lets the box go. The weight of the box swings it toward the wharf. The old man pulls hard on the rope. The box appears about to smash into the wharf. Its bottom is sagging under the 200 pounds of fish and ice. It rises over the edge of the wharf by a foot. Two men grab it in flight and swing it onto a large scale. One of the men takes the loops off the box; the other pushes the boom back over the boat where Matteo, hands hanging along his side, eyes turned impassively upward, waits.

# COMING IN, GOING HOME

Santo stands to the side of the old winch man. Santo's arms are crossed on his chest, his legs spread sturdily apart. It is the way he's been standing all day. It is the way he'd stand in a gale. He watches from that distance the jangling chaos of the dock workers as they heave and tug and curse at his fish.

Only they are not his fish anymore. They are things in a box being reduced to pounds: "Large cod . . . 194 pounds . . . get it outa here. What're you guys doing? Somebody get over here and get this thing outa here. . . . Wha'd'ya mean there's no place to put it? Where's the fucking jitterbug? God Almighty, three jitterbugs around here and nobody can find one. . . . Hold it! *Hold* it! Somebody get off their ass and find a jitterbug and get this shit outa here."

So that's what it is—shit. Twelve hours of fishing for shit. Large cod or shit, whiting or shit—what difference does it make? Santo doesn't care because the 194 pounds of shit is worth nearly $50 to him when it reaches the Fulton Fish Market in New York later that night, and there are nine more boxes just like it coming out of the hold. That's $450 from the cod-shit alone. That's the trip. Keep the shit coming. The boat made some money today.

Anthony straddles the starboard rail, his legs dangling on either side. He has a light fishing line and a hook which he drops over the side with no bait. He jigs the line, watches carefully, then lifts his arm quickly and hauls aboard a nice smelt maybe four inches long. He lays the smelt on the rail, looks up at the box swinging out of the hold toward the wharf, then goes back to fishing. Someday, maybe, he'll have to put up with those guys; someday he'll have to accept the reduction of the sacred cod to shit, but for now the hell with it, he'll just keep fishing.

"Hey, Santo. You talk to this guy." Santo looks up and

sees a small, slight, narrow-faced man coming at him. The man is dressed in a baby-blue, lightweight sport shirt. He has tan, double-knit pants, a broad, white, leather belt, and pointed shoes. His black, wavy hair is slicked back along the sides of his head. He wants to buy a box of shrimp.

Santo bows his head and listens. It seems this guy has a small stall in Haymarket Square in Boston. Oh, yes, it's very, very small. He does not do much business, but it keeps his nice family off the street, and he must have the shrimp. It sells so-so, he does not make much money from it, but some people, you know, they like it.

Santo listens as the man whines on. Santo looks the man over, quickly and accurately calculating the man's worth, figuring what a box of shrimp will bring on the market, adds $10 to his conclusion, and says, "$50."

Fifty dollars? Oh, no, no, no. That is too much. The man will go broke. Fifty dollars? Santo must understand: this is a small store; he is a little man. He was thinking, perhaps, $35.

Santo looks at him again. "$42."

This is awful. The man so needs the shrimp. It is not a big item, but the customers, it brings them in. They come back. They buy other fish. Even $42. The man must make a profit, just a little profit. "$37.50."

Santo, of course, understands the man's plight, but certainly the man understands, too, it is not just the shrimp but the box. The box costs $3. If the man will pay for the box he can have the shrimp for $40.

The man doesn't need the box. He has a barrel in his car. Santo nods and says, "All right. $37.50," but . . . the man must also pay the older guy in the gray workshirt two dollars for the use of the wharf.

The man reaches into his hip pocket and takes out a

wallet, opens it, and peels off three tens, a five, and two ones from the stash of green bills stuffed in the wallet. He digs into his front pocket and hauls out a handful of change, gives the $37 to Santo, finds two quarters, and gives him these, too, and puts the rest of the change and the wallet back in his pants. He starts to walk off.

"Hey," Santo says quietly. "For my friend here?" The man takes out two more dollar bills and gives them to the man in the gray workshirt, then walks to the scales where the shrimp have already been set aside.

Santo and the older man watch the small fish-stall owner tug the 200-pound box to his waiting late-model Buick. They smile.

"Here," the older man says. "Take it," and gives Santo the two dollars. Santo takes it.

"I woulda let him have it for $35," Santo says. "I'm not sure I could've gotten rid of it anywhere else."

"That's what I figured," the older man says. "He offered me $30, but I figured I'd let you see what you could do with him. He'll make his money back. Don't worry."

"I'm not," Santo says. "Those little salamis do all right."

"You can bet on it."

"That the last one?" the pock-faced man yells down to Matteo. Matteo nods. "O.K. That's it. Get the rest a this stuff inside. Get some empty boxes out here. . . . How many? Twenty-seven? Find twenty-seven boxes and make sure they're washed out."

There is a great rushing about. One jitterbug races out the main door of the warehouse with a skid piled high with empty boxes. A second forks through, the skid piled with the remaining full boxes of fish. Everyone is in a hurry;

nobody is watching what the other is doing. The jitterbug with the fish whirls around backward and starts forward toward the warehouse just as the other is passing in front of him.

"Look out," someone yells. Both hit their brakes. The empty boxes fly off the skid, a couple land corner down on the asphalt and are broken. One of the full boxes slides forward and begins to tip. Two men race for it and push it back on top.

"Pay some fucking attention," the pock-faced man screams.

"Up yours," one of the jitterbug jockeys hollers back.

"That's money you're dumping all over the place," the pock-faced man yells.

"Aagh," the jockey says, and races full tilt for the ware-house.

"Here they come. Who's catching down there? Come on."

Matteo waits. Anthony pulls up another smelt. Santo takes a slip of paper with the weights tabulated on it from the older man, looks it over, and sticks it in his breast pocket, then walks to the ladder and climbs carefully down to the boat below.

One by one the boxes are tossed down to Matteo, who catches them one hand on the side, the other on the bottom, and almost without looking passes them down into the hold to Mike, who stores them on either side under the deck.

"That's it, Santo. See you tomorrow," the older man yells down from the edge of the wharf. Everyone else has left. In the background is the electric hum of the two jitterbugs dashing around inside the warehouse loading Santo's fish into a large refrigerated truck backed half into the warehouse.

Santo nods, kicks the engine over. Anthony and Matteo flip the bow and stern lines off the wharf bollards and coil the lines as Santo eases the *Maureen* away, clears the last piling, turns her sharply to starboard, and heads across the inner harbor toward the Felicia Oil Wharf.

There are two women standing there when the *Maureen* takes its place among the other boats along the wharf. One woman is older, the other a teenager. Mother and daughter. They catch the lines Matteo and Anthony heave at them and walk them fore and aft and drop them around the bollards, then come back and stand looking down on the deck.

Santo turns off the engine, shuts the starboard window, and sits down on the bunk. He takes off his boots, places them neatly along the wall, and slides his feet into his shoes which have not been disturbed all day from the way he left them early that morning. He gets up, makes a final check of the wheelhouse, and leaves, locking the door behind him.

One after the other the men climb the wooden ladder to the wharf and stand by the two women. Both Mike and Matteo have plastic bags filled with shrimp and small haddock. Anthony holds a large lobster that had come up in one of the tows.

Slowly the four men and the two women walk down the wharf past the other boats moored there, silent, at rest.

The older woman turns to Santo. "Something happened to the car today. It started to smoke. I turned it off; now it won't start."

"That's all right," Santo says. "We'll take a look at it."

* * *

"I tell ya, these young kids get better looking every year. They didn't look that good when we was that age.

105

Jesus! Will you look at that. Ooo-oo." Tommy can't take his eyes off the two girls getting into the long white Olds parked in front of Steverino's Coffeeshop on Main Street. And they know it. They're taking a little too long getting in. "You know what it is, the blood's better. It's these mixed marriages. I knew I was doing right when I married the blonde. That French and German blood with all my guinea blood. My kids are a lot better looking than I am."

"Shit," says Busty in rebuttal. "That's nice stuff, though, and don't they know it." He takes off his Budweiser Beer hat and tips it to the two girls, who giggle, slam the door, and squeal away.

Nutzie is leaning back against the jukebox, a cigarette drooping from between his lips. He's still singing "Wha'd'ya want wit my goil? Wha'd'ya do wi . . ."

"Who's got a quarter?" Olly asks. "Somebody put some money in that thing." Nutzie laughs.

"All youse girls put money in, keep old Nutzie in business," Nutzie says. Nutzie used to have the jukebox concession in the West End of the city. He's given it up, but he likes the idea.

"Here's your coffees. Somebody pick 'em up," says a dark-haired, pretty girl in a white waitress dress behind the counter. "Which one of you is paying?"

"Olly's got it," says Busty.

"Tommy's buying," says Olly.

"I'm going broke keeping youse guys in coffee," Tommy says. "Here's the money. Somebody else is getting the coffee."

Olly rises slowly and brings the coffees to the table, passes them around, and goes back and buys a donut for himself.

"It's getting worse and worse. I don't know. Won't be

long before we're paying to go out and catch nothing," Tommy says.

"Heard Salvi got thirty boxes today. Wha'd Spava get?" Busty asks.

"How should I know? Who asks?" Tommy says.

"I did all right—six boxes gray sole. I don't understand why you guys keep after that fucking whiting. There's no money there. The greasers are cutting you outa the market," Olly says.

"And look what it's doing to your engine. You gotta run too slow; it'd kill my engine," Busty says. "Maybe we oughta go off Middle Bank for a time."

"Yeah, well, we gotta try something. I don't dare go home these days," Tommy says.

"Wha'd'ya do wit my goil? Wha'd'ya say to my . . ?" Nutzie sings on happily.

"Here's a quarter, play something," Olly says.

"Put on the Dean Martin thing," says Tommy. "There's a man that can sing."

"Tie a yellow ribbon round the old oak tree," the jukebox blares.

"Jesus, God! Tony Orlando. Where does a guy like that get off picking a guinea name like that?" says Tommy.

"I gotta go," says Olly. "Said I'd take the old lady out to supper tonight. Got to. My God, was she ripped last night."

"Yeah, I gotta go, too. Where you going tomorrow?" asks Busty.

"I don't know. You did all right today. Maybe I'll come your way," says Tommy.

"I guess I'll go back. . . . Well, four o'clock at Dunkin' Donuts." Busty swallows the rest of his coffee and leaves.

"Let's go, Nunu. The blonde's waiting. I'll take you

home," says Tommy. Nutzie squashes his old hat down on his head. "Wha'd'ya do wit my goil?" he sings, walking out the door.

"Jesus and Mary," says Olly. "Don't you know nothing more than that?"

"Wha'd'ya say to my goil. . . ?"

# 6

---

# *Friday—The Day of Rest*

**Y**ears ago there was a superstition among the fishermen that any boat going out on a Friday was certain to return to port with a "broker," a busted trip on which no one would make any money. That superstition was eventually abandoned (probably because too many nonbelievers made too much money).

Then there was a time when the fishermen, most being Catholic, stayed home on Friday and ate fish instead of catching them. That, too, was stopped, much to the detriment of the fishing industry as a whole.

The boats still do not go out fishing on Friday. The reason is pragmatic and persuasive. The Fulton Fish Market in New York, where most of the boats send their fish each afternoon, is closed on Saturday and Sunday. And where there is no market, there is no money; and when there is no money, fishermen do not fish.

* * *

The Fort is a knoll of granite which punches out like a fist at the more gracious shore of Rocky Neck. A channel runs between the two and connects the sheltered inner harbor with the broad and open outer harbor which reaches

111

past the Dogbar Breakwater, past Norman's Woe where the *Hesperus* spent her final hours, out to the fishing grounds. When the tide is in, three draggers can pass through the channel side by side and laugh. When the tide is out, they pay attention.

Straddling the Fort are several unpretentious, square, three-story, green, white, or brown houses inhabited now as they have been for years by Italians. Some people call the Fort the "Italian ghetto," for it was there that the Yankees, the Irish, and the Portuguese relegated the Italian fishermen who began immigrating from Boston, then in families from Sicily at the turn of the century. There is a story that once an Italian fisherman wandered from the Fort and got lost in the city and the police had to bring him home. It is said that he never wandered again. That is a Portuguese story. The Italians wander at will now. They are the fishing fleet. The Yankees, the Irish, and the Portuguese have all but left the waterfront, which begins, properly, at the Fort.

At the base of the Fort are a number of once-prosperous, now ramshackle fish-processing plants, as well as the Cape Pond Ice Co., where the boats ice up before going out. Next to Cape Pond Ice is Ocean Crest Seafoods, Inc., and next to Ocean Crest is Progressive Oil. Leo Linquata owns Ocean Crest. He also owns Progressive Oil, as well as Seven Seas Wharf farther around the inner harbor. A number of boats tie up at both Ocean Crest and Seven Seas Wharf and buy their fuel at Progressive Oil. They have to, even though they pay more for their fuel there than anywhere else in the city. There is a compelling reason: if they don't buy from Progressive, they had better look for space on another wharf—and there aren't many wharves left and even less space.

The boats at the next two wharves—Felicia Oil and

Frontiero Bros.—are confronted with the same restriction. In fact, there is only one place in the inner harbor where the boats can tie up and not be obligated also to buy fuel and that is the State Fish Pier, where there is no fuel and also no room.

Next to Frontiero Bros. is Harbor Cove, where the lobster boats moor, and where the Fort ends and the West End and Rogers Street begins. Rogers Street runs along the waterfront until it meets Main Street at the Gorton Corporation's main packing plant and new office building. On the left-hand side of Rogers Street in the West End there are the St. Peter's Club, then the Old Timers, then the House of Mitch, and a block later where Porter Street comes in there are Kelleher's and Joe's Dugout. There used to be more bars along Rogers Street, just as there used to be more fishing boats, more fishermen, and more wharves.

On the right-hand side, diagonally across from the House of Mitch, is Fisherman's Wharf. Fisherman's Wharf looks and smells the way the waterfront used to look and smell before the Russians discovered Georges Bank. Next to Fisherman's Wharf is Seven Seas Wharf on which the Gloucester House Restaurant is located. This is where the tourists come to take pictures of what's left of the world-famous fishing fleet.

For a quarter of a mile after Seven Seas Wharf there are no wharves. There used to be, but Urban Renewal has razed them. Where Madruga's Fish Co. once stood, there is barren land waiting for a Ramada Inn. Then there is the Gloucester Building Center where rotting pilings tell of the days long gone when lumber was delivered by barge. There is the Empire Fish Co., where boats tie up just long enough to take out a trip, then have to move elsewhere; the new Coast Guard station, where Bertolino's Fish Co. once stood;

and Sookie Sawyer's Lobster Pound; then the main office of the Gloucester Marine Railways, where one or two boats can tie up temporarily. And finally there is Star Fisheries. A few small draggers tie at Star.

After Star Fisheries there is the Quincy Market Cold Storage & Warehouse Co. at Rogers Street followed by Quincy Market Cold Storage & Warehouse Co. at Rowe Square, which is shared by Gorton's. Both facilities have long, concrete piers reserved for the oceangoing freighters from Norway, Denmark, Iceland, Scotland, and Japan carrying frozen fish, much of which was caught within 200 miles of the United States coastline.

Following Gorton's is a series of short slips along a new pier being built by Frank Rose III. The grandfather was one of the first of the Portuguese captains in Gloucester. The father is one of the last of the Portuguese captains. The son owns the largest oil company in the city. Beside Rose's Wharf is the A.D.E. Shrimp Co., a Swedish firm. Four small draggers tie up there.

Jutting into the inner harbor across from A.D.E. and Rose's is the State Fish Pier, built for the fishermen in 1938. It contains a large cold-storage and freezing plant, a fish-rendering plant, a herring-processing plant, and a set of small fish-processing stalls. Boats can tie up there if they are willing to move when another boat arrives with fish to take out which, for most of the year, happens every day.

After the State Fish Pier along East Main Street there are small wharves for pleasure boats; three boatyards; a third Quincy Market Cold Storage & Warehouse Co. facility, for freighters only; John Wright's Fish Co., with room for one small dragger; Morse & Sibley's Wharf, for gillnetters only (and Capt. Bill Sibley's small dragger *Peggy Belle*); moorings for sailboats; docks for yachts; and finally, around on the heel of Rocky Neck, the Gloucester Marine Railways second and major drydock. Ten to fifteen offshore draggers tie up at Gloucester Marine Railways.

Old engravings and photographs of the inner harbor show the waterfront from the Fort to the Gloucester Marine Railways on Rocky Neck teeming with masts and wharves and processing plants. That was when there were 300 to 400 boats in the fleet. Today there are at most 120 boats, counting lobster boats, and that number is diminishing by one or two each year.

But on Fridays that past appears to return. With the exception of those offshore draggers still on a trip, the boats are in, and at Felicia Oil, Frontiero Bros., Fisherman's Wharf, Seven Seas Wharf, Star Fisheries, Rose's, Morse & Sibley's, and Gloucester Marine Railways at Rocky Neck, nets are rolled out, a new cod end being laced on. The crew of the *Little Flower* is sitting on their rimwracked net, knives dangling open on strings from their belts or clenched between their teeth, needles wrapped with twine in one hand, cutting and mending. The crew of the *Alba* has stretched the two wires off the winch and has run them parallel the length of the wharf and is measuring off twenty-five-fathom sections with a six-foot stick, taping the mark, then driving a marlin spike between the strands, twisting open a hole, and stuffing white cord through. The crew of the *Acme* is switching nets, and the once-gray *Little Al* is being painted an eggshell blue which makes the boat look like the muscular brother of the *Lady In Blue* tied at Ocean Crest.

The *Little Al*'s crew hangs off the gallows, down over the bow. Two men balance on a small raft along the port side, painting the waterline. A half-consumed six-pack sits

on the forward hatch cover. Empty styrofoam coffee cups
float on the ebbing, oil-some tide with short ends of orange
twine and pieces of broken fish box lids.

The *Paul & Josephine* and the *Cape Cod* cast off for the
Cape Pond Ice Co. to ice up for Saturday. Santo Militello
emerges from the *Maureen*'s engine room after having
changed the oil, gets in his car, and drives to John Wright's
to pick up his stock receipts for the week, then goes to
Gloucester Marine Railways where he settles up.

Fishermen wander from boat to boat, stop and watch,
say something. There's a burst of laughter, a flurry of ges-
ticulating hands. A man working on a net has to have his
say, one of the *Little Al*'s painters disagrees, one of the *Alba*'s crew puts down his marlin spike and comes over to disagree with the disagreement. One of the *Acme*'s crew
says, "Mug up," and five men jam into a late-model Ford
sedan with a gold cross and a naked monkey dancing together from the rearview mirrow, and drive up to Sam's
Pastry Shop on Main Street for a coffee and Italian pastry.

The four-faced clock in the tower above City Hall reads
8:14 A.M.

\* \* \*

Joe Favazza is short, slight, and pale, almost delicate,
and he wears dark horn-rimmed glasses that won't hold on
his ears and keep sliding down his nose. He looks like a bank
clerk, acts like a bank clerk, and aside from the few years
he spent managing two RKO theaters in New Orleans some
time ago, that is what Joe has been most of his life—a bank
clerk, or, as Joe insists, a bored bank clerk.

Joe runs Fisherman's Wharf. The captains who tie up
there are the owners, but as they are out fishing most of the
week, the operation of the place falls to Joe. He likes it that

way. He is quiet, unassuming, and speaks with a faint "Y'all." He doesn't like crowds or confusion. He likes getting up and walking to work and ambling home when he wants to, and he likes the security of knowing that as long as he can keep Fisherman's Wharf turning a profit for the boys each year, no one is going to ask more of him. At forty-five or fifty-five, certainly no less, probably no more, Joe Favazza, the bank clerk from New Orleans, has found an unlikely home on the Gloucester waterfront.

Joe is standing behind his cluttered desk in his small, musty, cream-green office on the second floor of Fisherman's Wharf. He is tapping methodically on his calculator, adding up fuel receipts, ice receipts, grub receipts, supply receipts, repair bills, subtracting these from the stock receipts sent up from the Fulton Fish Market, dividing the total by the number of shares allotted the crew, the captain, the boat, punching and scribbling and entering it all on the form in front of him, making out the checks, folding the receipts in a packet, clipping them together and setting the checks in one pile, the receipts in another, and putting the form in a folder which he sticks in the big green file-cabinet drawer behind him and shoves shut.

This is what Joe does best—settling up. He has it down to a system. There are twelve boats he settles up for each Friday, and no settlement should take more than fifteen minutes. But most do. The damned captains always seem to forget something. They can never get all their slips together at the same time, and suddenly they're gone for half an hour, and there are all the other slips lying around the desk, and there are other boats waiting to be settled up. Everything should be done by noon because the captains want to get out of there and the boys need their money. It never fails.

And because the captains keep introducing chaos into his sense of order and procedure, Joe is always in a hurry, and that is one of the few things about the job that makes him sad. The hurry forces him to use the calculator.

"I wish I could do it all freehand. It would make it more . . . exciting," Joe says.

Settling up is not complicated. It takes a certain amount of patience, accuracy, and, well, understanding. Some of the men, like Spava Bertolino of the *Clinton,* do it themselves, but then Spava has a reason: he doesn't want anyone to know what he makes, especially his crew. Spava has a new house to pay for, and, while the crew doesn't know it, they are paying for that house. Some men have their wives settle up. One wife not only makes out the checks, but signs them with her husband's signature. His check is made out to him and is signed ostensibly by him. For awhile he was bold enough to endorse it himself. Now he has his wife endorse his name too. "I keep telling her she's going to get caught someday and end up in jail. She laughs," he says.

But having wives settle up is not common for one basic reason—"shack." Most fishermen and their wives have an agreement: he fishes and she takes care of everything else, in return for which he gives her everything he makes—except for a little bit he keeps out. That little bit is called "shack."

"Shack" is as old as the waterfront and its original meaning is clear: it was the money the fishermen didn't tell their wives about, just as they didn't tell their wives about the women they spent it on. At least that's the way it began. Today, "shack" is pocket money, mad money is how it is often described, to be spent on an evening with the old lady at Captain Courageous, an afternoon with the horses at

Suffolk Downs, or buying the bar for the boys at Mitch's.

The problem with "shack" is not that the wives don't see it, although they know it exists, but that neither does the government, and, as "shack" is taxable, the Internal Revenue Service has spent a great deal of time trying to get its part back.

Vito Favaloro of the *Anthony & Josephine* stands in front of Joe's desk. Vito is short and bull-shouldered and has a head of wild, black hair which he keeps trying to smooth back. For the past ten minutes he has been pacing back and forth between Joe's office and a small, locked closet in the meeting hall just off the office. In the closet is a bare lightbulb, a chair, a small table, and a telephone. For $60 a year Vito gets a key to the closet and the privilege of calling anywhere in the country free of charge. He's been calling his dealer in New York, trying to get the prices on two trips of fish he sent down earlier in the week. The dealer is being vague, so Vito has had to roughly estimate what he should be getting, and now he's ready to settle up.

He gives Joe a handful of checks and bills. Joe totals the checks. The *Anthony & Josephine* has stocked $3,356 for the week. Vito tells Joe, "Take a couple of hundred off that. The boys haven't seen nothing for a couple of weeks."

So now the *Anthony & Josephine* has stocked only $3,156 for the week, out of which come the bills. The remainder, minus taxes, is shared among the five crew members with the boat getting four and a half shares. This division is called the "Italian lay." Each crew member has a check for around $250, the captain has one for $325. There's an $816 check for the boat and a $116 check for Fisherman's Wharf for fuel and supplies. And there is a check for $200 made out to "Cash." When he gets around to it, Vito will cash the check and divide the $200 among

119

the crew. That is their "shack." It is undeclared money. No
taxes have been paid on it. It is up to each crew member
to pay those taxes. It's not much money. It's easy to forget.

Joe shrugs. He's been around the waterfront long
enough to appreciate the arguments that support things
like "shack." The best fishing season is almost over; winter
is coming and bringing down Nor'easters with it. There are
going to be weeks ahead when boats big and small aren't
going to be able to go out.

And Joe knows that tomorrow an engine could blow on
the *St. Mary,* or there could be a electrical fire like the one
on the *Baby Jerry* two days ago which will lay her up for
at least a month, during which no one on board will make
any money. And if it costs $2,000 just to haul and paint a
boat, what will a new engine or an entire new electrical
system cost? And last year was a bad year for fish, this year
has been worse, so what's next year to be like?

So the boys take what they can get when it's there, and
if there's something more on the side, finest kind, they get
that, too, if they can, because tomorrow it may not be there
and there'll be families to feed then just like now. And what
the hell, where does the "shack" come from?—the stock,
the fish they caught. It's all their money; they're just taking
it back.

"That's the way it is," Joe says as he clears his desk into
neat piles of slips and checks, shuts the door of the ancient
safe behind him, searches through his pants pocket until he
finds a key to the office door, and leaves, locking the door
behind him.

He walks through the waiting room past the large blackboard on which has been chalked the news that ice is is
going up to $16 a ton ($18 on weekends and holidays),

down the worn, creaking, unsure stairs to the ground floor, and out onto the wharf. He scarcely notices the men seated on the old plank bench leaning against the asphalt-shingled building, but instead heads down the wharf past the *St. Bernadette* where Tommy Aiello is trying to talk Peter Favazza (no relation) into cutting a piece of metal off one of Tommy's doors, past the *Francis R,* past the *Gicalone C* which Capt. Giovanni Gicalone has lashed to the wharf and is waiting for the tide to leave dry so he can cut out a line he fouled in the propellor, past the collection of doors the boys have left in scattered piles and the whalebone Salvi Testeverde dragged up in a tow, past the cars in the Captain Courageous parking lot, up Porter Street, to the bank.

In his pocket there is over ten thousand dollars in endorsed checks.

\* \* \*

There's a story going around the waterfront and Tommy is telling it.

It seems there are these two sisters and one has a husband who owns a dragger and the other has a husband who sits around the house and collects unemployment. So, the second sister asks the first if there is a site on the boat for her husband. There is, and apparently the husband gives up his unemployment and goes out fishing.

A couple of weeks later the second sister calls up the first and asks, "Don't that boat of your husband's ever settle up? Two weeks it's been and we haven't seen anything."

To which the first sister reportedly replied: "First, we get him out of the house. Now you want us to pay him, too?"

Tommy's been trying to tell that story for days and he's

finally found an audience in the storage room at the foot of the stairs under Joe's office. The storage room is low-ceilinged, heavily braced, painted penboard gray. Nets are lined up in mounds along the base of the walls. There is a stale smell of dried sea.

Some of the boys have gathered by the far door leading to the cold-storage area. They aren't saying much as they watch Turk Curcuru mend a net he has hooked to a nail driven into one of the hefty support columns. Turk's got his knife clenched in his teeth and he's staring at a hole in the net, trying to figure where he's to cut so the hole will be clean and he can start shuttling the needle and tieing the knots and filling the hole with an evenly spaced web of tiny mesh. He is scowling, which is why they call him Turk.

Turk doesn't think much of the story. The others know the husbands involved and agree it has to be true. This pleases Tommy and prompts him to take out of his pocket a petition he is circulating. The petition calls for the federal government to reclassify fishermen as "skilled" laborers. Hidden between the lines is an attempt to bring more Italian fishermen to Gloucester from Sicily to fill the vacant sites on the offshore draggers. There is a shortage of offshore fishermen because few Gloucester men are willing to spend two weeks away from home at one time.

"Wha' da we want any more greasers for? There's too fucking many of 'em already," Turk says.

"Shut up and read the thing," Tommy answers. "You see what it says? It says we're unskilled. Minga!"

The boys feel some sort of obligation to sign. They've never thought of themselves as unskilled, and if that's what the feds say they are, well, "Fuck the bastards. Let those fat cocks come down here and take one of these boats out and try to catch fish. They'd never make it past the breakwater. We'd have to go out and save their assess. I'd let 'em drown, the whole fucking bunch of 'em.''

The boys don't think much of the federal government and they suspect the feeling is mutual. So, they'll sign it, not so more "greasers" can fish in Gloucester, but because who are those guys to call the fishermen "unskilled."

While they are signing it and passing it on, Spava Bertolino joins them. That is, he stands in the doorway a few feet away, hands on hips, shoulders back, chin out, and says, "Wha' da youse boys thinking on the shrimpers?"

Spava is not popular with the boys and normally they wouldn't give his questions much time, but the shrimpers have them worried. The processors aren't giving any sort of price for the shrimp being landed. In the last week the price has dropped ten cents, and to top that the processors are taking thirty percent off the top as trash, shrimp too small or soft to go through the machines. As a result the shrimpers are collecting on only seventy percent of their catch and they're not making any money.

That's fine with the boys because most of the shrimpers are "greasers" and the "greasers" are too greedy and now it's catching up with them. The only trouble is, the shrimpers are switching over to whiting, which is the staple of the boys' market. So far it hasn't been a good year. The fish haven't appeared the way they have in the past. Still, the price in New York has stayed steady at $10 to $14 a hundredweight all summer and everyone has been making money. But with the shrimpers cutting into the market there is bound to be a glut and the price is going to fall.

"I don't want youse boys to worry," Tommy says. "I got it all worked out. They're going to go out and catch all our whiting and they're going to let us stay in and carry picket signs for them. Now that's friendly, ain't it?"

"Fuck those guys," Turk offers. "They gotta go after shrimp. They got too much money tied up in those boats. I'll tell youse, those guys stay away from shrimp too long, there's going to be a lot of eighty-footers for sale."

That seems to settle it. Spava walks off. Turk takes the net off the hook and drops it in a pile, folds the blade into his knife, pockets it, and leaves. Tommy turns to his brother Nutzie and says, "Let's go home. Momma's got lunch waiting for us."

So Tommy, who has five children, and Nutzie, who has five children, and are themselves from a family of five children, go off up the wharf to the weekly family lunch at Momma's.

\* \* \*

Up on Porter Street at the side entrance to Joe's Dugout, Busty Frontiero is standing with his cousin Sammy of the longliner *Sweet Sue,* Sammy Orlando of the *St. Bernadette,* and a couple of men from the *Santa Lucia.* Busty is holding forth, and when Busty holds forth, the boys let him because, while Busty has kind, laughing eyes and a seemingly even disposition, he is also big and he has a thick black mustache which is menacing when he closes his mouth and shuts the twinkle out of his eyes.

Busty has a problem. It's with his dealer in New York. The guy has been screwing him and Busty is tired of it. Getting screwed is part of the business. Every dealer does it and every fisherman gets it, but sometimes it goes too far and something has to be done, and Busty is warming up to do it. He's about to switch dealers.

It's a hard thing to do because fishermen are creatures of habit. Their life is rigorous enough and they like it to be as routine as possible. It's enough to catch the fish. They

don't want to be bothered with the selling. They would like
to think they can trust their dealers, but they know they
can't. Still, they give them as much slack line as they dare
because, well, it's like their wives, if they can't trust them
to be honest while they're away, they'll go crazy worrying
and they won't be able to concentrate on fishing.

The dealers (and the wives) know this, and, while both
depend on the fishermen for their livelihood, the dealers
take more liberties than the wives do. And for men like
Busty and Tommy, Olly, Santo, Spava, and most of the
inshore fleet, the problem is compounded by the fact they
rarely, if ever, meet their dealers face-to-face. One is in New
York, the other is in Gloucester, and only sometimes do the
dealers come up. Even then it is never a direct business
confrontation, but more of a courtship, with the dealers on
their best behavior, buying meals here, drinks there, and in
some cases setting aside a little "gift" for a color television
the fisherman may have wanted but couldn't see his way to
buying.

Otherwise, all business is transacted over the telephone,
and rarely with the dealer himself but usually with someone
skilled in calming irate fishermen looking for an honest
price for their fish. And, of course, once the fish leaves the
wharf and the truck is on the road to New York, the fishermen are completely at the mercy of the dealer. Tommy
Aiello explains it this way:

"Years ago I started out dealing with this guy in New
York. Then, he was renting an apartment in Brooklyn, and
he didn't dare walk the streets there were so many bookies
looking for him. Then one day he's got a place in Queens
and he's driving a secondhand Cadillac. Now, he lives some
place on Long Island, and he's got a pool and a new Continental. And I'm still driving my old, beat-to-shit Chevy."

125

"Someday," Tommy adds, "we're all going to die and we're all going to 'that place.' And you know what's going to happen? I'll tell youse—we're going to be taken to a giant stadium and all the fishermen are going to be given seats in the stands. Then the dealers are going to be paraded out on the field and the fishermen are going to stand up and turn thumbs down, and those bastards are going to roast."

That's the way Busty is feeling as he leans against the hood of a parked car and waxes on his subject. It seems that last week he was checking over the receipts sent up from New York and he spotted an "error." For his yellow-tail flounder he'd been given a price of 1¢. Now yellow-tails have been holding steady all summer at 16¢, regardless of the dealer, and no matter what kind of glut might have hit the New York Market the price could not have dropped to 1¢ in a day. Obviously it was an error in New York. A bookkeeper had just "forgotten" to add the six, and certainly they were very sorry and it would never happen again. But Busty knows, they all know, that if Busty hadn't found the "error," no one in New York would have mentioned it, and the dealer would have had himself 200 pounds of yellow-tails for $2 instead of the $32 he owed, and on the wholesale markup of at least fifty percent that would have been a hell of a day's profit—at Busty's expense.

That's the kind of thing that has been going on recently. So Busty called on Wednesday and told them that the fish that was coming down was the last fish they'd be seeing from him.

Busty dramatically draws a twice-folded, well-sat-upon envelope out of his hip pocket and takes from it his receipts for the last two shipments. The boys gather around and begin to laugh. The receipts show that on Tuesday Busty sent down twelve boxes of whiting. Each box weighs approximately 125 pounds, yet the receipt shows a total weight of 1,600 pounds, one hundred more than could be expected. Besides that, he's been given 12¢ a pound when the best he's been doing all summer is between 8¢ and 10¢. And the same thing happened Wednesday with ten boxes being weighed out at 1,400 pounds at 14¢.

"How the fuck'r you s'posed to deal with guys like that?" Busty asks. "I don't care what they give me now. I'm changing."

Everyone agrees. There's even a fleeting embarrassment for the dealer who has reduced himself to such blatant bribery. It's almost like not playing by the rules, but what can you expect? Sammy Orlando is about to lay out his woes when a stranger arrives and starts pressing a small, yellow card in everyone's hand.

The stranger is a slight, handsome, young Italian, casually, but well dressed, and the card he's pushing introduces him as a "deaf person selling these cards for a living. PAY ANY PRICE. Thank you for your kindness." On the flip side are sixteen hand signs for things like: good, bad, hi, nice, sweetheart, marry, and no good.

"How you doing?" Busty asks. The man shakes his head and waggles his index finger back and forth in front of his mouth, supposedly indicating that he can't understand a word that's being said to him.

"Haven't I seen you before?" asks cousin Sammy. Again the waggling finger.

It's an awkward moment. Everyone knows the guy is a fake, but there is always the outside chance he is what he pretends to be, and if he is, no one wants to be the one who turned him away. Yet no one wants to be taken either, for no matter how much they give him, it's blood money and you give that to your friends, not to hype artists.

But who's going to be the first to be suckered? Busty tries again and when he gets the waggling finger, he says, "Fuck him," and digs into his pocket and comes up with a quarter. That starts the flow, and the professional deaf mute shakes everybody's hand and walks off up Porter Street a dollar and a half richer.

Cousin Sammy looks at the yellow PAY ANY PRICE card he's still holding in his land and drops it on the ground. He starts to laugh.

"Remember that guy down at Fisherman's Wharf a couple weeks ago when he came in right in the middle of the skin show, and everybody gave him something to get rid of him?" Sammy says.

"Yeah," says Busty, "And Nutzie tells him to shut the door when he's leaving . . . and he does. Shit . . . ! I'll buy you boys a drink."

\* \* \*

Johnny LaTassa is a great bartender. Big and hefty, with black, curly hair, he is almost unobtrusive. He doesn't try to be one of the boys because he already is. There is nothing about the waterfront he doesn't know, but he doesn't gossip. There is a certainty about Johnny that you could tell him anything and be confident that at least a day would pass before it became public; and, when it did, nobody would recall how they had learned it nor would they care, because it would seem by then to be general information.

Johnny doesn't like standing behind the bar, but prefers to wander around the House of Mitch, or Mitch's, as it is more properly called, or Michelle's to the intimates. Sometimes he sits down on one of the bar stools and talks with the boys, or leans back in one of the chairs at the table that butts against the wall of the small kitchen and studies the track results in the *Herald-American* sports section, then gazes out the front door at the cars passing on Rogers Street or at the help at Captain Courageous across the street taking supplies off a delivery truck, or nods to those passing by who nod at him.

Or he'll stand looking over the continual pool game going on in the backroom, and mostly he'll keep his mouth shut while the boys play. But once in a while he'll say something, almost aside, and whoever is shooting would do well to listen because Johnny speaks as one who has seen a lot of pool and could probably run the table once and again if tested.

Or he'll disappear into the kitchen and nobody'll know he's gone. The boys will go behind the bar and mix their own drinks, and if anyone else wants a drink, whoever is back there will mix that one up, too; and if no one can remember what a rum and Coke costs, someone will yell, "What's a rum and Coke?" and Johnny will come to the door of the kitchen and quietly tell, then disappear again.

And when he emerges at last he may have a plate full of tuna fish sandwiches wrapped in cellophane or ham-and-cheese sandwiches, and these he'll put on the bar. He'll go back in again and return with a platter of tongues and cheeks or scallops or strips of fried squid or fried whiting or hake, which he'll arbitrarily put down in front of someone at the bar or stick on a long table set up in the rear of Mitch's, with paper plates and sliced, fresh Italian bread. The sandwiches you pay for, the fried fish is on the house. Johnny knows someone.

And the boys will ease over and load some of the fried fish onto a plate and come back to the bar or one of the booths or to the pool table. And there will be one smart-mouth who'll complain that the scallops aren't scallops but punched out skate wings, and Johnny will simply say, "Don't eat 'em." The smart-mouth does.

And when there is nothing else to do, Johnny will get a broom and sweep the place out, making the boys raise first one foot, then the other, on down the line as he sweeps the length of the bar. And only then does he go back behind the bar and lean against the bottle-lined shelf beside the hanging collection of old Massachusetts license plates, rest his arms on the tops of the bottles, stick one foot up on a case of beer, and with an amused look, survey his flock before him.

* * *

Teddy O'Neil is drinking his lunch and talking in slightly slurred earnest with Chubby Loiacano of the *Hunter.* Olly Palazolla of the *Sea Buddy* is standing behind Chubby, who, though only a year older, is Olly's uncle. Busty is seated next to Chubby and is arguing with Tommy Randazza of the *Pepe* whether there is or is not a hump on the 95-fathom line when you tow to the southeast toward Half Way Rock.

Olly is worried, not about humps because he doens't fish off Half Way Rock, but about Teddy O'Neil. Not that Olly minds a man drinking, but when Teddy starts he tends to keep at it all day, which is how Olly would prefer to see Teddy work on the *Sea Buddy*'s engine. A firefighter by night, Teddy moonlights as a mechanic by day and there is no one better in the city when he's sober. That morning Teddy got down to the boat late, took off a few parts, then had to go somewhere, and now here he is at Mitch's. At this rate, the chances of having the engine ready to go out at four o'clock tomorrow morning are diminishing, and, to make matters worse, Uncle Chubby has just bought the bar, which means a fresh drink sits in front of Teddy.

"Mother of fucking Christ, Teddy. I gotta go out to-morrow," Olly says. "What is this shit?"

"Whaaa? Oll-ly, you worry too much. You'll go out tomorrow. I'm promising you. I do what I say. You'll go out," Teddy says.

"I'd better," Olly says, watching Teddy move into the new drink. "Fuck it," Olly mumbles as he passes by Busty. Busty pinches him on the butt and tells him to sit down and relax. So he misses a day, what's he losing?

"Y'know what gray sole is bringing in New York? Seventy-five cents a pound. Eighty cents. Two weeks ago they was at ninety cents. Nine-ty fucking cents, Busty, 'cause there's none around. Who's catching 'em? Who ya know that's got any gray sole in the last month? No one but me. I'm catching good . . . and this clown's tieing me up 'cause he can't lay off the juice."

"Where you fishing, you got gray sole?" Busty asks. "I can't find nothing. The fish are all on the inside. They're not coming out like they should this time of year. I can't figure it."

"That's where you gotta go, Busty," Olly says. "You gotta go inside for 'em."

"I don't know. I don't like taking that chance, not the way I've been catching. You get caught, you got that $1,500 fine and there's the week, and maybe you lose your license, too. I don't know. I get scared inside."

"Yeah, Busty, but where's the fish? You don't go inside for 'em, you're gonna starve . . . and you know what I heard on the radio this morning? They've lost the *Jesse*. She went out yesterday and nobody knows where she is. Last thing they heard she's outa fuel and her batteries are run down, and she's caught up in a thicka fog. What kinda luck is that? *Natural Resources* is lost at sea so I got the whole inside to myself and my engine's spread out all over my boat. Sonuvabitch!"

"I should have your troubles," Busty says.

"Hey, you big salami, you playing or you hiding?" Cousin Sammy is at the far end of the pool table where he has just stuck a quarter into the slot and the balls are rumbling down the channel under the table.

"Minga! 'Big salami,' he calls me, this kid," Busty says to Tommy Randazza. "Yeah, I'm playing. Best outa three, loser buys the round."

"Play 'em one at a time. You buy as you lose," says Sammy, rolling the cue ball to the end of the table and racking the balls, centering the 8-ball in the point, spacing the solids and stripes, and rolling the frame around on the felt to tuck the balls in tight for the break.

Sammy's reputed to be a helluva pool player. He's got the quiet, serious, easy-to-smile but slow-to-laugh disposition that allows him to take his time, to line up the shot, to think ahead where he wants to leave the cue ball, and to stroke gently, just enough. He does not play as though a ball has to splinter when it hits the pocket.

But Busty's no mark either, although he's liable to let muscle take care of what a few seconds more consideration might manage equally well.

Busty picks up his drink and his cigarette and walks them to the end of the bar, brushes aside a couple of empty glasses, sets his drink down, then walks over to the cue-stick rack and selects his stick. Sammy, on the other hand, has his own cue stick locked in a cabinet fixed on the wall beside the rack. He digs into his pocket, finds the key, opens the cabinet door, and takes out a finely tapered cue stick which he screws together, sights down its length, and bends a couple of times before snatching the chalk off the table and working the tip of the stick into it.

Sammy breaks and sinks the 2-ball and the 13-ball, decides to go with the stripes and nudges his second shot to the lip of the far-corner pocket. It hangs there. Busty laughs, puts his vodka and ginger down, chalks his stick, bends over the table, and proceeds to run off a string of four balls before taking a long shot with the 6-ball in the far-right pocket, missing it, and leaving Sammy with a clean shot on the hanger.

One of the crew of the *Sea Witch II* goes over to the jukebox, finds the most jangling record on it, yells "Like that, Busty?" then dances to the buffet table, grabs a handful of fried hake, and returns to stand by the pool table. Olly takes a seat next to one of the *St. Peter III*'s crew at a small, round table against the near wall, clanks his drink down, and stretches out his legs which nearly reach under the pool table.

Chubby gets behind Sammy, who's lining up his shot, and advises him not to try it. Sammy sinks the shot, tries to maneuver for the 15-ball in the side, bumps into Chubby, and tells him to move his dumb guinea ass. Busty tells Chubby to stick with Sammy—he needs help. Sammy blows the 15-ball. Chubby retreats quickly back to the bar.

But that's the last one Sammy blows, and after Busty sinks the 6-ball but scratches while doing it, Sammy drops four in a row leaving him the 17-ball and then the 8-ball.

"In the side with the 9, Busty. It's your shot," says Olly as Busty steadies for the 6-ball off the 17-ball in the near-side pocket. Busty glances at the 9-ball, decides against it, but loses his concentration. He strokes too hard. The 6-ball hits the 17-ball flush, sending it off the cushion, leaving a straight shot for Sammy in the far side which, if he's careful, sets him up for the 8-ball in the far-left pocket for the game —and the drink.

Johnny LaTassa leans over the edge of the bar, grabs a couple of empty beer bottles, a dirty glass, and empties one ashtray into another. He takes a damp cloth and sweeps it over that part of the bar, then yells to Sammy, "What'r you drinking?"

"Vodka and ginger. For me," Busty answers. "On Sammy."

"Your ass," says Sammy, lining up the 17-ball. He strokes it gently with a soft, reverse spin. The 17-ball drops easily, the cue ball stops dead, all in a line for the 8-ball.

"I got Busty next," says Olly.

"Fuck you, you do," says Chubby. "He's mine today."

But Busty is already heading to the rack, keeping one eye on Sammy, who calmly bounces the 8-ball around the corner pocket and leaves it hanging. The boys quickly look into their drinks. Busty tries to keep a straight face.

He takes back his cue stick, walks to the table, shaking his head and repeating over and over: "You shouldn't play pool if you freeze on the 8 . . . you shouldn't play pool if you freeze on the 8," and neatly sinks his last three balls, and there's the 8-ball hanging like an apple in Eden. He lines up the shot, hesitates, looks up at Sammy, and says, "Big salami, eh? You dumb guinea," and then rolls the cue ball teasingly along the cushion and the 8-ball disappears.

"C'mon, cousin. One more," Busty says, but Sammy has already unscrewed his stick and has locked it up in the cabinet. He takes five dollars out of his wallet and lays it on the bar.

"Who's the big salami, cousin?" Busty asks as he picks up his fresh vodka and ginger by Sammy's elbow and resumes his seat next to Tommy Randazza.

". . . And you know why you never seen that hump," Busty says as though he had never left. "I been thinking. You come into the 95-line from the outside. Right?"

\* \* \*

Philly Verga is looking good. With white-white shoes, light-blue, double-knit slacks, a broad white leather belt with a white buckle, and a matching, blue open-neck sport shirt, his black, wavy hair slicked back, his thin, swarthy, chisled face shaved and braced, Philly's got action in mind. He sits down next to his *compare* Chubby, puts his arm around him, catches Johnny's eye and points to Chubby's half-filled glass, calls for a whiskey on the rocks, begins to laugh, and announces to Chubby that he has just "packed my clothes."

To which Chubby says, "No shit."

Philly says he had to. It seems that the owner of the boat was loading the grub bill, and while that would have been all right, he was also not giving any "shack" and that was not all right. Philly has been around the waterfront too long. He didn't like the smell of what was going on.

For loading the grub bill is an old trick owners and captains resort to when they need a little money to make ends meet. It doesn't happen often with the inshore boats on which the grub usually consists of a cup of coffee, a donut, and a sliced-ham sandwich for the full twelve hours out. But on the offshore draggers the grub bill can be as much as one hundred dollars a man for the ten-day trip. For, besides fishing and sleeping, eating is the only recreation the men have, and they insist on eating well.

The trick works this way: when a boat lands its trip, the entire catch is paid for and the captain takes the check.

Depending on the captain, he may or may not tell the crew how much the trip was worth. Whatever the amount, it is divided sixty percent for the crew and forty percent for the boat. Out of the crew's total share come those expenses which pertain specifically to them—food, ice, and fuel. All the rest—repairs on the engine, repairs on the boat, repairs on the electronic equipment, rope, twine, nets, buoys, rollers, plus insurance on both the boat and the crew—fall to the boat. This division is called the "lay," or, properly, the profit-sharing lay system. And while there are variations such as the "clear 40 lay," the "broken 40 lay," or, as is most common among the inshore fleet, the "Italian lay," the fishermen and the owners are married to it. The only alternative is a straight-salary arrangement, and a couple of "brokers" could tie the boat up for good. With the "lay" system, everybody makes money or no one does.

Almost. The problem with the "lay" is that, while the crew's expenses are somewhat fixed, they are minimal compared with the boat's expenses, which are also fixed; and of late the costs of maintaining the boats have doubled and in some cases tripled, while the boats have grown older and more in want of repairs. Consequently, many boat owners, if they are not also the captains, are making no more on a trip than the individual members of their crew, and often less. It is estimated that at least eighty percent of the boats over sixty feet long—or half the fleet—are for sale, if the price is right. And the price is dropping. One owner has devalued his boat for insurance purposes three times in the last three years, from $125,000 to $40,000. He says he would sell her at $60,000 and walk away singing.

In the past when owners found themselves going under, they simply paid the captain and the crew to sink the boat. One day the boat would go out and not come back. Miraculously, all hands would be saved without a scratch; there always seemed to be another boat standing by when she began to take on water or caught fire. Even more amazing, all the expensive electronic equipment would be saved, too, and, as often as not, new nets and doors would have been forgotten on that particular trip and would be safe on the wharf.

At the perfunctory Coast Guard hearing the captain and crew would pinpoint the accident miles from where the boat had actually gone down. Insurance companies wearied of trying to recover nonexistent boats in three hundred fathoms of water. The owners collected fully on their lost boats, bought another, and were in business again. A number of insurance companies went broke trying to keep up with the sinkings. Those companies that remained solvent either ceased insuring the boats or raised the premiums so high that the owners went broke trying to pay them. As a result, most of the inshore boats no longer carry insurance on either their boats or the crew. Their insurance against personal-injury suits is almost infallible; they only hire family as crew, and family members do not sue each other. If something happens to the boat, it is lost. Fortunately, very few boats have sunk in the last ten years. The offshore boats are denied their recourse. The crews are too large and there is a limit to the number of fishermen a family can produce. And, as the risk of danger is much greater, the crews are insured but the boats are often so devaluated that there is no profit in sinking them.

Caught between rising expenses and the loss of their most sure and rewarding escape route, some owners in financial trouble turn to less creditable ruses to stay afloat, and loading the grub bill falls among the least. Since all bills are sent to the owner and the crew rarely sees them, it is simple to add on an extra $100, divide it five or six ways, dock each man $25, and pay for the twine or the rent on the Loran.

As long as the crew is making money, they will not complain. They may grumble, but grumbling is as much a part of fishing as damp oilskins. They understand. If the owner is taking something off the top, if he's short-weighing the catch or pocketing the rebate on the fuel because expenses are draining him, it is in the crew's best interest to pretend they don't know what is going on. For their livelihood depends on the boat. Their lives hang on the boat's having sound equipment, having enough twine to mend the nets, enough nets to be able to keep fishing if one rimwracks on the tow and is too ripped up to repair on the spot.

But when they see money going from their pockets into the owner's and the boat is going from good to bad to worse, that's when they pack their clothes.

And Philly has been watching. He knows that one of the maxims of fishing is being abused. The owners of the boat died recently and the captain who inherited her has come down sick and can no longer fish, so he's hired a captain to take her out.

That is bad. If the owner can't be aboard, sell. If he doesn't, the boat will go to hell because there is no one around to care, no one to notice the little things like a worn shackle, a parting footrope, a rotting boom, a corroded gallows brace. When the owner is captain and he sees something that should be taken care of, he does it himself or tells the crew to do it *now*, and no one goes ashore until it is fixed. But an owner can't tell a captain what to do. Captains are touchy; they'll walk off the boat if the owner gets in the way. But a captain who is not the owner is no more than one of the crew, and when the boat is in after two weeks out fishing, he has no more interest in staying around the boat than the crew does. So little repairs are put off until the boat goes out again, and they're forgotten on the way out and put off the next time the boat is in. And one day the shackle breaks and someone is hurt, or the gallows lets go and the boat has to come in and maybe it has to lay up for a month, and a minor expense becomes a major debt.

That's what Philly has seen happening. The owner was already in debt to Star Fisheries, where the boat had taken its fish out for years, but she had to go on the ways and the owner had turned to Leo Linquata for a large loan. It was desperation that made him do it because not only does Leo own Seven Seas Wharf, he also owns Ocean Crest Seafoods, and Ocean Crest is bigger than Star Fisheries—and so is the loan. The boat now takes out at Ocean Crest and ties up at Seven Seas Wharf. It will be some time before Star Fisheries sees its money.

That's a sign things are deteriorating, that it's time to pack the clothes, and that is what Philly has done.

". . . And the bastard told me if I left, he'd make sure I couldn't collect no social" (unemployment), Philly tells Chubby, laughs, and sips at his whiskey. "And I tell him he can fuck the social, I got three sites already."

A week later the boat sank at the wharf. Someone, it is said, forgot to tighten the seacock before going ashore. Initially everyone concluded that she had been sunk for the insurance and that suspicion gained support from the rounds the captain bought for the boys later in the day at Kelleher's. Only there was no insurance on her. That's how far she had sunk.

* * *

"Y'see what I see?" Busty whispers to Olly.

"Jee-zus!" says Olly. "Look at that," he whispers to Chubby. Chubby looks up and elbows Philly, who's watching the crew of the *Lady In Blue* play pool. Philly turns around and can't believe it either.

"We gotta do something," Philly says.

"We gotta bust his balls," Busty states.

"That's it," Olly agrees. Chubby has already swung off his stool and is standing, beer in hand.

Booty Loiacano is in trouble. Besides being Chubby's brother and Olly's uncle and Philly's *compare,* he has just walked into Mitch's with not one, but two girls. Busty knows them. Their names are Stella and Gail.

Booty looks like a recently retired jockey—short, wiry, and dressed in a dark-blue T-shirt and new blue jeans. He's a number one fisherman when he's sober, a generous drinking companion when he's not. Right now he is rimwrack drunk. He has to be or he never would have brought the girls to Mitch's.

Not that it's unwise to bring girls to Mitch's, they come all the time, it's just unwise for Booty because Booty has gotten out of hand too often in the past with other men's girls, and now here he is with two of his own. No one can believe it.

Busty gathers in his two drinks (the pool table has been good to him) and starts for the table by the cigarette machine and the side door where Booty has tried to secrete the girls. The boys are with him. This is going to be better than Sammy freezing on the 8-ball.

There's an empty seat next to Gail and Busty slides into it. There are no more chairs so Chubby swings three over from the adjoining table, takes one, Sammy another, Olly the third, and Philly wedges himself between the cigarette machine and Busty, hoists himself up on top of the machine, and rests his feet on the back of Busty's chair. Some of the other boys in the bar want to help and pull the chairless table up behind Booty and sit on it.

Busty opens by saying hello to the girls, who hello him back, then he starts on Booty, who is trying to talk to Stella, who in turn is smiling at Busty.

"Booty, you old dog, you trying to ignore your old friends?" Busty asks. "Here you are and you won't come over and be friendly. You gotta sit over here like you're ashamed. You ashamed of us, Booty?"

Booty ignores him, tries to turn himself around enough that his back is to everyone but Stella, but no matter how he turns there is someone hanging on his shoulder.

"Boo-ty," the boys chant imploringly. "Boo-ty, be friendly. Introduce us."

"Will you guys . . ?" Booty snaps, but he can't finish because Busty has already begun to introduce the girls.

"Stella, this is Olly. Olly . . . Stella, Gail. Gail, Stella . . . that's Chubby, that's Philly. Sammy, you know Stella, Gail," and so on until everyone knows everyone. All the boys stand up and shake the girls' hands, each time bumping against Booty, pushing him further and further off his chair into the table. And like a drowning man whose every gulp for air is met with a smothering wave, Booty keeps spluttering, "Will you guys fuck off," which the boys agree is not nice talk in front of women and each apologizes for Booty. And when the girls begin to giggle, that's enough for Booty, who wants to push his chair back and get out of there, but can't because there are too many feet on it and the chair won't budge.

Busty calls for drinks around and the boys say that Booty can't leave when someone is buying a drink for him.

141

But Booty says he'll buy his own and, with a Herculean shove, forces enough space to free himself, and with the agility of a cornered mouse, squirms past the entanglement of legs, bodies, and chairs to safety and a stool at the bar.

There's a miner's rush for the empty chair, which Sammy wins. Johnny yells from the bar that somebody'd better get the drinks. Chubby does, brings them over and sets them on the table, spilling part of one on a book Gail has just taken out of the public library. After the jacket has been wiped dry, each of the boys picks it up and looks it over, then looks at Gail, at Stella, and wonders aloud why anyone reads this stuff. The book is about a girl named Stella who is insane in a variety of ways. Gail says she thinks it's very interesting. Her tone is mildly condescending, suggesting she has been in better places before. The fact is, she lives with a fisherman named Kenny, who should be in soon and is liable to beat her if she is too friendly with the boys. And the way she's looking at Busty, she could be very friendly.

Meanwhile, Booty is at the bar burning, trying to figure a way of slipping Stella from the barricade of bodies the boys have thrown up around her. The drink he has in his hand has brought down a thickening fog, but he can still see enough ahead to realize a frontal attack would only lose him more ground.

His opening comes when Gail decides Busty isn't worth the beating and excuses herself, which leaves Stella. And since the boys do not seem to be paying any attention to her, Booty catches her eye and, with an imperial wave, signals her to join him. Which she does with an "I've got to go to the bathroom." No one is about to doubt her.

With Stella gone, Busty starts laughing and recalls the time a girl named Ralph came into Mitch's and Booty had been unsinkable. Nothing the boys could say would calm him down. So Busty had told her the next time Booty did something she didn't like to belt him and not to worry, they'd all be right behind her.

Now Ralph wasn't called Ralph because her mother thought it was cute, so Busty's advice was thoughtfully given, and no sooner had Booty started in again than he found himself going backward over his chair and sliding down the cigarette machine into a pile on the floor, receiving for his troubles an egg from the machine and a rose on his cheek the size of Ralph's fist. That ended Ralph's problems for the afternoon.

But Booty learns slowly and Ralph's lesson had been quickly forgotten. Therefore, the boys are determined that this time Booty will come to understand. Only they must be careful. Booty is angry. He's losing control. He may start swinging. And no one is supposed to get hurt.

One by one they return to the bar and gather around Booty. Busty gives Stella a quarter and tells her to find something on the jukebox. When she gets up, Olly takes her place, Busty sits on Booty's other side, Chubby and Philly stand in close behind, and together they begin ordering drinks—on Booty.

"No one's on Booty," Booty starts yelling. "Booty's on Booty . . . Booty's on Booty."

Chubby winks at Johnny and says, "Don't listen to him. He doesn't know what he's saying. Vodka and ginger, whiskey on the rocks, two beers—on my brother here."

"Fuck you," says Booty. "I'm not paying nothing. You guineas buy your own."

"That's not nice, goumba," says Philly. "We buy you a drink, you don't buy us nothing. That's not class, goumba."

Johnny sets the drinks up and walks off. Philly picks

Booty's wallet and, before Booty can grab it back, Philly takes a $5 bill and lays it on the bar. Booty reaches for it, but Olly slides the bill away. With an ungracious "shit," Booty squirms off his stool and goes over to the pool table, drink in hand, and sulks.

It isn't like Booty not to buy the bar. The boys conclude that, for what it has all been worth, Booty's balls have been busted. His sulking has taken the fun out of the game, and now he's saying something to Stella and she looks as though she's going to cry.

Busty goes over to Booty, puts his arm around him, and suggests the two of them take on the winners of the pool game in progress. They should be pigeons. Only a bunch of gillnetters. Minga! Look at 'em. Riffraff. No class.

Busty is serious, but Booty refuses the partnership, instead grabs Stella by the meat of her arm, and marches her past the bar and out the Rogers Street door.

"Hey, goumba, come back. It's all over."

"Boo-ty, it was for fun, uncle."

"C'mon, brother, we'll buy you a drink."

"Booty, don't be a hard-ass."

"Fuck you!"

* * *

Day is night and night is day, and weeks and months and seasons pass by Joe's Dugout with no more recognition than the daily changing of the guard behind the long, highly polished bar.

Olly ducks off Porter Street down three steps and shoves open the wooden door and steps further down to the dark tile floor which is almost black by the door because that's the end of the main room and there is hardly any light for the booths back there, only that which seeps around the partition walling off the Men's Room in the far corner. Faces and bodies materialize as his eyes adjust. There's a pool table in the center of the room with two directed lights hanging over it, and two men standing back in the semi-darkness watching a third bending over the table lining up a shot. And along the near wall running with the street above is a plastic couch and half a dozen bodies leaning on, stretching out over, and sitting on it, mugs of beer and bottles and glasses scattered between legs and hips and feet.

Along the far wall are highbacked booths with small, glass, imitation ship lanterns for each. One booth is empty. An old drunk named Billy sits in the second muttering. In the third, two fishermen off an offshore dragger and a young girl, braless in a white turtleneck and flowing plaid skirt, negotiate.

The bar is at the far end. It stretches the width of the room and there are bright-orange plastic stools with backs and aluminum legs. They are all taken.

The bar is stopped at the far end by a partition separating the main room from a side room, and leaning against the partition is a tall, heavyset man in a pink shirt and white pants with a light-green belt holding the two together on his hump of a stomach. He has one hand cupped under the stern of a girl known simply as Stiff. In his other hand is a highball and he's waving it around and talking loudly at a big, fat man who is covering the next stool and staring at Stiff's stomach which is spilling out from a gap left by her tight, cut-off, blue jean shorts and her skin-tight, blue and white, thin-striped T-shirt.

Olly doesn't waste time looking around for anyone he knows. He twists past the bending-over pool player, turns right at the cigarette machine, and enters the side-room, where he is hit full in the face by a bank of smoke being blown through the opening by a large fan stuck in the far corner. There's a loud "Oll-lee."

"Oll-lee. Where you been, Olly? Give the kid a seat. Move over, goumba, the kid wants to sit down."

That's Nutzie, back from lunch at Mamma's, and Nutzie is being unabashedly Nutzie, underplayed, outrageous, comic, slouching his small self into the plastic seat that runs along the wall separating the side room from the main room, cradling his beer in his lap, and whistling his words around the few teeth that remain in his mouth which is roundly open in a world-wide grin. No one takes Nutzie seriously. He won't let them. But there is no hiding the wisdom of the fool.

"What's news?" Olly says, taking the chair Sammy Orlando has shoved into place for him, turning it around and sitting in it backward, resting his arms across the top of the back.

"You want news, you buy the beers," says Nutzie. "How many we got here? One, two, three, four . . . whaaa! No? You're drinking, Salvi. Olly's paying." (Salvi Testeverde has been trying to leave for the last half-hour. He's got to buy some large manila envelopes to send something to family in Sicily and the only reason he hasn't gone is he's trying to figure if he can get away with cutting up a shopping bag instead.) ". . . Four, and five. Five cold beers. Carole, five beers for these nice girls."

"Wha'd'ya want now?" shrills Carole, sticking her head around the partition that divides the long bar from the short second bar and yelling between two fortyish women squared away on stools at the bar. "Ya want more, you guys clean that foul-looking table first," and she throws a damp rag down on a tray.

The boys like Carole because in her way she is like the

sea. She blows up like the devil with indigestion, but, if they can weather her, she blows out to a flat-assed calm and the clumsiest flattery will realize drinks on the house.

So there's a flurry of movement. The three tables the boys have commandeered are suddenly spotless and, bythe time the last empty mug is back on the bar, Carole has returned with the five frosted replacements.

They're a strange-looking bunch. Besides Olly, at thirty-six the youngest, and Nutzie, the jester, there is Tommy, short like his brother, a little leaner, dressed as always in loose-fitting, dark-green pants and matching shirt and a tired black baseball hat that covers his thinning, still-black hair. Tommy is the "sea lawyer" with certain knowledge on all subjects and a willingness to share it all with anyone who will listen, which includes about everyone except Nutzie, who quietly laughs while his brother proclaims.

And there's Salvi Testeverde. Rosario Salvatore Testeverde of the *Linda B.* Broad and heavy and tough, with an enormous, almost ferocious head and tight, curly, whitening hair. Salvi, they say, is like his dog. He'll lick you to death one day and rip you apart the next. His *compare* Spava Bertolino calls him "Dr. Jackle and Dr. Hyde."

And there's Sammy Orlando of the *St. Bernadette,* who has his nephew Joey with him. Sammy is lean like Olly, but not as imposingly strong. He's wearing a new blue yachting cap and a shocking-clean, dark-brown workshirt, and, while he is usually taciturn, today he's bleak. For Sammy is hurting all over. That morning he'd had a tooth pulled, he's got raging hemorrhoids, and now he's got to listen to his nephew complain that the kid's mother, Sammy's sister, is nagging the kid that Sammy doesn't pay him enough. That's too much to take.

". . . And you can tell your mother she can mind her own goddamned business. When you're worth more, I'll pay you more. I'm running a fishing boat, not a . . . a . . ."

"I know, uncle. That's what I keep telling her, but she says . . ."

"I don't give a shit what she says. You don't know what you're doing out there. Maybe you'll learn. Depends on what you want to do. But until you show me you want to fish, you're only worth a quarter-share and you can tell your mother I'm being generous with that."

"I tell her, but she keeps saying that without my dad you woulda . . ."

"Fuck your dad. Ask her how many times I had to wake him outa bed. And you wanta know what really happened that time by the bridge? Ah, Mother of Jesus, tell your mother she's got some complaint, t' see me. I don't want you involved in this thing. You know what I mean?"

"I know, Uncle Sammy. I know. I keep telling her, but you know how she is."

"Yeah, I know . . . Jesus!" Sammy squirms on his chair in pain.

"I thought you got those things fixed this morning," Salvi says.

"No, I got the tooth pulled. Jesus Christ! The thing hurt like a bastard yesterday. Had to come in early it was so bad, and the fucking dentist says he can't do nothing till next week. I tell him this thing's got to come out, I can't fish. So he says for me to come in this morning, he'll do something."

"That's what I'm saying," Salvi continues. "It's like the Italian who went to the dentist to get his tooth pulled and the dentist yanks and yanks and nothing comes. And he yanks some more and finally the thing gives and out comes the tooth with a long string and he pulls the long string out and there at the end's the guy's balls."

Sammy can't laugh, but Tommy sees his opening.

"There were these three doctors and they're telling each other what their favorite patients are. One says he likes the Irish 'cause they've got so much whiskey in them all the parts are perfectly preserved. The next says he likes the French because they're so small all the parts are miniature and easy to work on. The third says he prefers the Italians because they've only got two parts—the mouth and the asshole—and they're interchangeable."

"I had a Portuguee worked for me once and he'd bleed so bad that after clearing the deck his pants would be stiff." Salvi is feeling good. "You know what he'd do? He'd get a bucket and fill it with ice and he'd take down his pants right there on the deck and sit on the bucket till the bleeding stopped."

Sammy says he doesn't bleed anymore, that he's past that, and the boys agree Sammy is in trouble, and he'd better have the things cut right the hell out. But it's right in the middle of summer, the best fishing season, and it would be three weeks before he could get fishing again and there's no one around who'd take his boat out and he can't afford to tie her up now.

Which reminds Sammy he owes Salvi and apology because the day before he'd given Salvi some bad information while they were fishing together off the Isle of Shoals and he doesn't want Salvi to think he's like other fishermen and lies to his friends.

"Salvi, as God is my witness, I'm sorry. You know I'd never tell you wrong. You gotta believe me."

Salvi is astounded. He doesn't know what Sammy's talking about.

"I told you I had four boxes, I had nine. I didn't know."

Salvi raises his hand. Say no more. But Sammy is a penitent. His heart sags with guilt. The hemmorhoids are suddenly a crown of thorns.

"I looked. I saw nothing but trash. I thought, 'Four boxes,' and I couldn't have been more surprised when I see nine boxes and I said to myself—God strike me if I'm lying —'I told my *compare* Salvi wrong and when he sees what I've got at the wharf, he's going to say, "That Sammy, he lies to me." ' "

Sammy's contrition is too heavy for even Salvi to bear. "That's all right, goumba. We make mistakes. I was catching good anyway, so I'm glad you got fish. Forget it. I buy you a drink."

"What's this, Salvi? You get soft when you grow old?" Olly says. "Maybe you're trying to find new bottom to fish?"

"Listen how this salami speaks. Without Tommy and Busty to show you around, you wouldn't be nowhere now. You'd have your boat for sale."

This is vintage Salvi, the face turning red, the veins in the neck bulging, rising up and leaning across the table. A younger Salvi might have gone right across it, but now he lets Nutzie pull him back into his seat from which he stares at Olly and, chin high, dismisses him with a "Pfff."

Olly laughs, and, like a dog on a weary grizzly, he charges again.

"You're too old, Salvi. You've forgotten too much bottom. Too long you've fished the same place. No you can't remember the old marks. You can't move. Now you got to come to me."

Salvi heaves from his seat. "You know what? You don't know. You don't know nothing but what Tommy's shown you. You know what you better do? You better get down on your hands and knees and kiss Tommy's ass."

"He knows," Tommy says quickly. "That's why he calls me, 'Baba.' He knows what I done for him. Now he shows me marks. He learns good. Maybe you could learn from him, Salvi."

"Yeah, Salvi. You come with me. We'll fish together. I'll show you bottom you've never seen before."

"When I do that, I tie up my boat," says an unsoothed but exhausted Salvi. He takes a long swallow, puts his beer down, takes out his wallet, lays five dollars on the table, and says, "Someone get these boys more beer. I go home. Tomorrow I go fishing . . ."

# PART II

## The Offshore Fleet

# 1

## Going Out

The fishing dragger *Joseph & Lucia III* stands at the end of the wharf, her lines still fast. On board, the crew wanders the deck checking loose gear, tying it down before the boat puts to sea. Below, in the hold, the hold man is filling the last pen with crushed ice that rushes down from a large black hose stretched across the deck from a small shack on the edge of the long, wooden wharf.

Forward, in the galley, the cook is making up the first pot of coffee, and while he waits for it to boil on the black, cast-iron stove, he stores the last of the supplies that have been brought aboard.

Aft, in the engine room, the chief engineer is cleaning up the small workbench, rubbing a grease stain off the floor. Beside him, the spotless, gray, 600-horsepower diesel is silent.

The captain is in the pilot house leaning over a chart table in the far corner of the chart room, a pencil in one hand, calipers in the other. A radio is blaring. The dial is set to an uninterrupted marine forecast. Every few minutes the forecaster reports that the waters off Gloucester Harbor are calm with winds between 0 and 10 miles per hour. The captain glances up at the wind gauge fixed to the back wall.

The gauge reads 20 miles per hour. He goes back to studying the chart. When the forecaster announces a storm developing off the Carolinas heading northeast with gale-force winds predicted, the captain turns off the small overhanging lamp and enters the pilot house and looks down on deck.

A small yellow car backs slowly down the length of the wharf and stops about twenty feet from the boat. A short heavyset woman in an overcoat gets out and walks to the edge. She stands there hands in her pockets, and looks up at the pilot house window.

"Tommy," she calls. "Tommy." She calls it patiently.

The captain opens the front port window and sticks his head out.

"What do you want?" he asks.

"It's bad weather out, Tommy. Stay in another day."

"What do you mean, bad weather? You call this bad weather?"

"Tommy, they're calling for a storm. Why not stay in and see? Just one day. See."

"Go home. Get in that car and go home. I'll see you when we get in."

"Tommy . . ."

"Go home."

"Good-bye, Tommy. Call me."

"Yah. Good-bye." He pulls the window shut.

"Have a good trip," she says.

And she walks to her car, gets in, and drives back up the long wharf, up the hill, turns left onto Harbor Loop, and disappears . . .

To the big yellow house on Addison Street and goes quickly to the kitchen where she putters about cleaning up, never straying too far from the Citizen's Band radio which sits on the counter by the refrigerator.

156

And she waits for the call which most of the time never comes. But every once in awhile—it may be two, three hours later—she'll hear "Tina . . . Tina." And she'll grab for the receiver.

"Come down and get me."

Then she'll laugh and say, "I told you . . . and you could have been home all the time."

And Tommy will say, "I didn't call to hear you talk . . . get down and pick me up."

It's a ritual they've gone through for almost thirty years.

\* \* \*

Captain Tommy Brancaleone stands in the pilot house of the *Joseph & Lucia III,* one hand on the stainless-steel gear fixed on the counter that runs the width of the bridge.

Below him, the black snake of a hose still lies on the deck, lifeless. No more ice spills from it. Gaspar Palazzolo, the hold man, climbs through the hatch and pulls the heavy iron cover over it, fastening it down tight.

On the bow over the doghouse, Santo Aloi stands solemnly, staring down the wharf at the city. An idle, expressionless stare. He waits for the bow lines to be cast off.

"Get that thing off the deck. Let's get outa here," Tommy yells through the open pilot house window, and at once his eldest son Joe Charley appears along the port side and begins to haul the black hose to the rail. A man in the small shed on the edge of the wharf reaches down to help, and the hose is raised up and laid by the shed.

"Get those lines," Joe Charley says to the man.

"Jesus, you guys are always in a big hurry. Take it easy," the man says, walking slowly toward the stern where he pulls in some slack from the stern line, slips the loop off the wharf bollard, and hands the line down.

"Get the other line," Tommy yells.

"Easy, Cap," the man says. "We'll get there. Take it easy."

Santo hauls in the bow line and the boat is free of the wharf. It may be two weeks before she is made fast again.

Slowly Tommy eases the gear into reverse. The boat moves backward. His hand moves from the throttle to the hydraulic stearing gear. The stern eases to port. As it begins to nudge at the heavy pilings of the wharf, Tommy pushes the throttle forward and reverses the steering gear, swinging the bow slightly to starboard. The stern runs along the edge of the wharf, barely missing the pilings as the bow gradually begins to point out toward the channel. Tommy advances the throttle further. The boat trembles. Off the stern a froth is stirred up by the propellor beneath. The bow begins its 270° arc, slowly leaving Star Fishery, then Quincy Market & Cold Storage, then the State Fish Pier, then Smith's Cove and the rise of East Gloucester, then the Rocky Neck Railways to port.

And at last the *Joseph & Lucia III* is in midchannel, steaming by the Coast Guard station, Empire Fish Co., the Building Center, the Gloucester House, Fisherman's Wharf, Captain Courageous, Harbor Cove, Frontiero Bros., Felicia Oil, Ocean Crest Sea Food, the Cape Pond Ice Co., Producer's Fish Co., Curcuru Fish Co.—all to starboard—and to port, the Rocky Neck Artist Colony, then the Tarr & Wonson Ltd. Marine Paint Co.

It's 9:30, Saturday morning, and there is a damp winter chill on the city. A few cars run along Rogers Street. There is a feeling of snow or freezing rain.

The inner harbor is ruffled by small chop and the outer

harbor is cold grey, and there is ice on the rocks of Ten Pound Island and a gull's seated on top of the red channel light. And as the *Joseph & Lucia III* passes out of the inner into the outer harbor and picks up speed, passing by the red and black channel buoys, the long, grey granite span of the Dogbar Breakwater comes into view. And, every so often, a wave from the rolling grey, white-fringed sea outside breaks over it, sending up a spray that settles over the breakwater into the still, now-empty mooring area for the Eastern Point Yacht Club.

Before the *Joseph & Lucia III* reaches the breakwater, she begins to pitch forward, not much, just enough to make Tommy spread his feet and lean back against the wall of the pilot house, not enough to make him reach for the oak support rod fixed to the ceiling. His arms are crossed on his chest.

With him is his brother Tony, the engineer. Tony is two years younger than the captain but looks older. He sits in a swivel stool by the port window, one arm resting on the sill, the other hanging lightly over the throttle. He is leaning forward toward the window, rocking easily back and forth with the slow pitching of the boat, his eyes surveying the deck below, then rising and gazing out at the nearing ocean swells.

Neither man says anything. The weather forecaster continues his endless marine forecast. His voice, scratched by the static of the radio, seems to be screaming over the dull roar of diesel below. His forecast has not changed for the past hour. He persists in reporting two- to three-foot seas and 0 to 10 winds off Gloucester Harbor.

The two men stare out the window as the boat rounds past the breakwater. Their faces are impassive. The seas are running four to five feet and the wind gauge shows 20 to 25, with gusts from the northeast up to 30.

In front of them is unbroken ocean. Stretching out on both sides is nothing but cresting, rolling sea. Behind the boat, the Dogbar Breakwater, the rocky cliff shore of Magnolia with its pine and hemlock and granite covering, and the large wood and stone houses set firmly against the winds. And the breakers working over Norman's Woe where a long time ago the *Hesperus* foundered, and off the stern to port the shores of Eastern Point stretching past the craggy Back Shore with its run of large motels, past Good Harbor Beach and Briar Neck and Long Beach, and reaching off toward Rockport, and ending with the twin towers on Thacher Island. Out of sight to the starboard, lost in the heavy grey overcast of the morning, is the skyline of Boston, two and a half hours' steaming away.

And far off the bows to the starboard: Georges Bank, Cultivator Shoal, Sharrers Ridge; to port: Brown's Bank, Grand Manan Bank, Sable Island, and closer Jefferys Ledge and Bigelow's Bight. The fishing grounds. One boat with 26,000 square miles of fishing grounds to choose from. Two weeks of fishing ahead.

"We're going for a killing," says Tommy and heads the boat directly into the Nor'easter.

One hundred eighty miles away, in the mouth of the Bay of Fundy, lie the Grand Manan Banks, and within the Grand Manan Banks sit the Southwest Banks and the Northeast Banks. A year before there were gray sole off Southwest Bank, and in Boston the price was high. Last trip, the price on grey sole was high again; the question is whether the gray sole are back on Southwest Bank. If they are, everybody will make money. If they're not . . . well, it's a day's steaming up to find out, and there are redfish off Northeast Bank.

For the first time the bow digs into the oncoming sea, the boat rolls and twists through the belly of the swell, and the wave breaks over the peak. Sliced in half by the wedge of the bow, it rises up like a curtain and is blown by the headwind the length of the boat. For a moment all visibility in the pilot house is obscured, then it runs in sheets down the windows, revealing below the decks awash with sea running out the scuppers.

Tommy leans forward to brace himself against the shelf on which the compass and the controls sit. He waits for the boat to right itself, then moves quickly to his swivel chair on the starboard side. He sits down, braces his feet against the baseboard heater that runs along the front wall of the pilot house, leans back, and prepares to wait out the next twenty-four hours of bucking to the grounds.

The trip is beginning and the weather is about what can be expected in the Northwest Atlantic in the middle of winter. It could be worse. It could be 0 to 10 winds and a light, running sea, and that would bring out the rest of the offshore fleet. As long as it stays bad, the other boats will stay in, and that will be just fine when the fish reach Boston and go up for auction. The fewer the boats, the fewer the fish . . . and the better the price.

"Ride 'em, cowboy," says Tommy. He's smiling.

# 2

## Reaching the Grounds

Grand Manan Banks. Twenty hours steaming out of Gloucester into a winter Nor'easter, and, in the first light of the gray breaking dawn, the thin layer of ice covering the boat looks like fresh varnish.

The windows of the pilot house are steamed, and Joe Charley, seated in the captain's swivel chair, rubs clear a spot on the forward window, yawns, looks out over the plunging bows seventy feet in front of him, and sees nothing but gray sky over gray rolling, whitecapped seas running in tangled swells over the banks a hundred fathoms below.

He looks up at the brass ship's clock on the rear wall. It reads 5:36 a.m. He checks the two Lorans behind him, then lights up a cigarette from the nearly empty pack on the shelf beside him.

He stands up, stretches, shakes his head a couple of times, and, grabbing for the doorjambs for support as the boat is jolted by a breaking wave, he moves through the doorway to the chart room and stands at the head of the ladder leading down to the captain's stateroom.

"I guess we're about there, Cap," he says in a soft voice, then returns to the captain's stool and again rubs the spot on the window clear.

163

A minute later Tommy comes through the doorway into the pilot house, still pulling up his thick, green wool pants and taking a hitch in his belt. He sees Joe Charley and barks, "What's the matter with your own stool?"

And without a word, Joe Charley picks up his cigarettes and moves to the port stool while Tommy leans over and peers into the Loran, then falls into his swivel stool.

"Anyone around?" Tommy asks.

"Not that I could see," Joe Charley answers. "Nothing all night."

"Well, they're all to the southward, with Nino, I suppose. We got the place all to ourselves. Now we gotta set on some fish."

"Guess that's right, Cap . . . should I wake the men?"

"Let 'em sleep . . . we won't be setting out for a couple hours yet."

"Whatever you say, Cap," and Joe Charley cups his head in his hands and goes back to staring out the window.

\* \* \*

Forward in the forecastle, Gil Roderick, the cook, rolls over onto his back and opens his eyes. He lies there staring sleep-dumb at the bottom of the bunk above him. Slowly he works his legs free from the worn brown blanket twisted around him and drops them over the edge of the bunk and sits up, his legs dangling just above the wood bench that runs between the bunks and galley table to a point in the bow under an old television hung from the ceiling.

Gil sits there, crouched over, swaying with the rolling of the boat as it lurches to starboard coming off the side of a swell passing below, then bucks back as the following wave lays a cross into the bow. He grabs the edge of the bunk with one hand, holding on, while with the other he

164

wipes the few strands of hair on his balding head out of his eyes. As the boat starts down the backside of the swell, Gil hoists himself from the bunk down onto the bench, slips his legs under the table, and shifts his way aft toward the galley.

As he stands up, the boat rises and comes down flat on a wave and pitches forward, sending him back down on the bench.

"Goddamn it . . . slow the fuck up!" he grumbles, and stands up again.

For forty of his fifty-eight years Gil has been a fisherman —cook, deckhand, hold man, even engineer—and he has never come to friendly terms with a bucking boat. He takes it personally that there is one thing that can disturb the easy equilibrium which is his trademark.

Slightly bent over, legs spread, he makes his way the ten feet aft to the galley stove, holding first to the steel post by the ladder which leads to the doghouse on deck, then to the framing of the open locker where the black oilskins hang and the black rubber boots lie flopped over on each other.

He reaches down and turns up the fan in front of the black cast-iron stove. The small oil-fed flame in the well of the stove flares and begins to whirl around the well under the cooking surface. There are two coffee pots on the surface. He takes one and slowly makes his way along the counter to the sink by the stainless-steel walk-in refrigerator built into the starboard wall. He pours out the remains of yesterday's black-brown, overcooked, still-lukewarm coffee, swishes clean water around in the pot, fills it to the top line, then shuffles his way back to the stove where he adds fresh grounds, puts on the lid, and sets it on the stove.

On the counter next to the stove lies a pound of bacon, put there the evening before to thaw so the slices can be easily peeled off. He finds a large frying pan and lays all the slices in the pan and sets it next to the coffeepot. Almost immediately the bacon begins to sizzle.

Abruptly the boat heaves to starboard, catching Gil too relaxed, sending him racing with little steps fighting for balance back toward the refrigerator, his hands grabbing at the edge of the counter like drags to slow him down. He stops in front of the sink and catches a glimpse of himself in the mirror over the sink and watches his face grimace as the boat corrects and wants to drag him back to port. But he has a firm grasp on the sink, and, when the boat evens off, he pulls open the heavy refrigerator door. Balancing himself against the frame of the door, he reaches in for a carton of eggs. Which he pulls out just before the steel door slams shut. Gil shuffles uphill toward the stove, his baggy gray pants, cuffs now under his heels, pulled half-down over his stern, the tails of his checkered shirt now hanging.

Already the relative coolness of the night in the forecastle is being driven out by the heat of the stove; and the nighttime silence once disturbed only by the rattling of the dishes, the clanging of pans in the cupboards, and the constant tremor of the engine at work aft, is broken by the whir of the fan over the stove. And beads of sweat break out on Gil's pale forehead where the strands of hair now stick.

Gil forks the slices of bacon over in the gathering grease, turns down the oil flow for the stove, and makes his way back to his bunk. Kneeling on the bench, he leans in and from a rack along the hull pulls out a catalogue of woodworking tools. He is about to turn around and sit at the galley table when there is a loud crack off the port bow; the boat seems to rise out of the water and be carried sideways. For a split second Gil is in the air. He ducks his head inside his bunk, grabbing onto the edge, and holds on while the boat jumps back on course.

Pulling his head back out he glances aft as though at the pilot house. "What's the big, fucking hurry?" he mumbles, and turns around and settles himself at the galley table, elbows on opposing edges of the open magazine. "Don't that man ever slow down?"

\* \* \*

It seems impossible, but Santo Aloi is snoring. He's lying flat on his back, with one leg draped out of his blanket and over the edge of his bunk, his head cupped in his hands, his weather-carved face relaxed in total quietude, his long body rolling imperceptibly with the boat. He looks like someone asleep in a rowboat in the middle of a placid pond just lazying the day away. The only thing missing is a fishing rod and an old straw hat.

Santo has the fisherman's facility for sleeping anytime, anywhere, for five minutes, half an hour, three hours, in a gale of wind or a flat-assed calm; and then to awaken and be on deck at three in the morning in a blizzard, to haul the nets back, mend the net, clean the fish, and be back in bed and sound asleep as though the whole thing were nothing but a dream. It's all part of the twenty-four-hour day on-duty life the fishermen live for eight, ten, fourteen days at a stretch. And Santo is a fisherman.

Santo looks like a man who would snore. He has a protruding nose on a lean, long, craggy face. His hair is stiff, wiry, and thinning, combed mostly with his long fingers which resemble galvanized spikes. He is tall for a fisherman, maybe a shade over six feet, and strong like a slave. His body appears sculpted from granite. He has the mien of a volcano that has remained dormant too long.

Santo does not talk much, and when he does it's in short bursts which come out with effort. He has a low, baritone voice that is close to a growl and perhaps it is the effort required to bring the words forth but his tone seems laced with an inner anger.

Santo surrounds himself with order. Both the bunk he sleeps in and the upper bunk in which he stores his few shipboard possessions are neat, his clothes laid out in piles as though he were always on the verge of packing a suitcase.

It is hard to know what Santo thinks about anything. He can become almost voluble on things like the difference between American and Italian coffee, but he will not enter debates on politics and his face is passive when questions of religion come up. But he reads tirelessly, cover to cover and back through again and again his collection of *Stop* magazines, a fifty-cent Italian cross between *Playboy* and the *National Inquirer* with a soupçon of *True Romance*. He reads them without a trace of emotion or any inclination to share their contents (most of which have already been given the once-over by the crew—and dismissed).

Santo's taciturnity is comparable in depth to the truculence of his "goumbatti," Gaspare Palazzolo, who is also dead asleep in the lower bunk across the forecastle.

Gaspare Palazzolo. "That's P-a-l-a-z-z-o-l-o, pronounced 'Pal-atz-o-lo,' " with the accent on the first *o*. For Gaspare this is very important because, while Gaspare is an American citizen, he is Italian first and forever, and one of the ways he can, in his own mind at least, maintain this distinction is by retaining the true spelling and pronunciation of his last name and not bastardizing it the way all the other Palazzolas or Pallazzollas or Palazolas or Palazollas in the city have. He has also kept the *e* on Gaspare. And he has almost conscientiously not learned to speak much English, although one suspects he knows and understands and could probably use more English than he shows.

Gaspare is fastidious, sometimes to the point of being prissy. He is the one member of the crew who, if seen on the street, would not be taken for a fisherman. He stands just under six feet tall and has strong shoulders and an almost rectangular figure, that is, there is a straight line down from the tips of his shoulders to the edge of his hips. And while he is not fat, he is not lean either and someday, should he ever stop fishing and take up a life on shore, he might become fat.

But what sets Gaspare apart is the almost sweet softness of his face which seems to have defied the erosion of years of days and nights on deck at sea. Only the heavy, dark stubble which gives his shaven face a bluish appearance and the prematurely white streaks in his thick, curly black hair support his contention that he is thirty-seven years old and has three children, one of whom, a son, is fifteen.

Gaspare has designed his life to include as few surprises and upheavals as possible. His motto is: "I try to do the best I can."

He lives in a large, square, moderately expensive, reasonably old house at 103 Prospect Street at the foot of Portuguee Hill. It could, but doesn't, overlook the harbor because there is a bigger house just below it. The house is immaculately white, with aluminum siding and a white picket fence that runs around three sides. The front door is maple and freshly varnished, and there is a polished brass nameplate beside the door.

But the front door is rarely used. Everyone uses the back door, which leads to the kitchen. This makes sense because the front door leads to the living room, and, while it is a large and well furnished, if traditional and cold, living room, it is seldom used. As in many of the Italian fishermen's homes it is a showplace. The children are never allowed in it, save to pass through on their way to the front stairs which lead to their bedroom. But the kitchen is used. It is where his wife and his mother-in-law hang out when they are not busy cleaning and polishing the rest of the house. It, too, is immaculate.

Everything about Gaspare is immaculate, in place, and free from as much contamination as can be kept outside the pale of his life. He himself succeeds in isolation by never taking a vacation and always fishing miles offshore.

And he keeps his wife—or she allows herself to be kept —as much as possible within the four walls of his house while he is gone. She goes outside to shop or to church— and she has been seen a few times on Main Street looking in clothing stores. But aside from such forays she remains tethered. He has not encouraged her—nor has she tried on her own—to get a license for the one family car. Only when he is in from a trip does she venture outside the city limits —or outside a walking radius of the house. Then she and Gaspare may go for a drive in the country, or, more probably, to one of the shopping centers twenty miles up Route 128.

Gaspare candidly admits that this is the way he wants it, this is the way he remembers it when he was young, and this is the way he became the person he is today. He finds no uneasiness in stating that "I am king in my own house. I work hard for it. I give them everything they need," so that when he is home he will be waited on, he will be served, he will snap fingers and people will act accordingly, and there will be no backtalk, no alternatives; and if there are, one sharp blow from his heavy right hand reduces the alternatives to a "yes, father."

But authoritarian as he is, the one thing he cannot control by sheer domination is the sea, and invariably he gets sick if the boat bucks on the way to the grounds.

And though he doesn't look it at the moment, stretched out so peacefully in his bunk, his blanket wrapped securely around him, he has been up periodically all night. Closer inspection reveals an ashen face and, given the rigidity of his body, the neatness of his blanket and the wooden bunk surrounding him, one needs to only stretch the imagination an inch to see a corpse.

* * *

"Breakfast, boys," Gil yells.

He's leaning over the galley table setting the coffeepot in the middle, next to a pan filled with partially burned toast.

(The boys say that Gil used to be a helluva cook, but something happened; Gil says it's "these goddamned guineas, they can't taste anything anyway. Give 'em spaghetti and butter and they're happy.")

"Breakfast time, Gaspare. Time to eat," Gil says.

He can see from Gaspare's white face it's been a long night. He also knows that Gaspare likes to eat.

Gil walks to the boat's telephone hung on the wall of the oilskins' locker in front of the stove and rings three times for the engine room where Tony and Joe Charley sleep.

"Breakfast, Chiefo . . . yah, that's right," and hangs up. Next he rings once for the pilot house. "Breakfast, Cap," and hangs up again.

And goes over to the sink and turns on the radio which is on a shelf to the right of it and gets a traffic report from Boston carried to sea in a soft, female voice. The *Joseph & Lucia III* may be 180 miles from port, fifty miles from land, not another boat in sight for miles in any direction, and winds blowing at 35 miles per hour with seas running six to eight feet, but for what it's worth, the Southeast Expressway is light with no slowups or accidents to report. Then a reliable male voice announces that during the night there was a gangland-style murder of an Everett man in Medford, a two-alarm fire in Sommerville, a racial incident at South Boston High, and the economic index shows no near end to the recession . . . with more news to come . . .

Gil isn't really listening. Nor are Gaspare and Santo as they crawl from their bunks and sit for a moment on the edge gathering themselves into the morning.

The boat suddenly slows and the pitching becomes a rocking. The dull roar of the engine dies down. There is a moment of repose which lasts for less than a minute, then the roar picks up and the boat lurches to starboard and Gil says, "Goddamn it," and seems to run downhill with the plate of hot bacon in his hand.

And there is the sound of feet coming down the ladder and Tony, the chief engineer known on board as "Chiefo," appears, followed by Joe Charley.

Tony is a small man, five feet six inches at the outside, but broad and compact, although a little on the soft side. And he has a gentle, passive, and rather sad face. There is something of the Seven Dwarfs about him. He has on a World War II navy jacket and an old, army-surplus aviator's hat with flapping earmuffs. And a heavy sweater under the jacket, and baggy green pants and boots.

"Good morning, good morning, good morning," he says,

pulling off the cap and throwing it on the shelf under the medicine cabinet.

"Good morning, Chiefo," Gil answers, then asks where the boat is.

"We're there," Tony says. "Guess we'll set out in a little while now."

"He figures around nine o'clock," Joe Charley says, taking off his red, grease-stained parka and throwing it onto Gil's bunk, then sliding himself up the bench to his spot halfway up the table. He bends far over the table and picks up an orange which he quarters and devours quickly. Almost in the same motion he grabs a slice of toast, wipes his knife on a paper towel, and cuts off a large chunk of butter which he spreads over the toast, folds the toast in half, in three bites consuming the entire thing, and sits back ready for breakfast.

Joe Charley has on a heavy undershirt beneath a checkered cotton shirt. He, too, has the thick, dark-green wool pants, baggy from the waist down. And workmen's boots. He has broad shoulders and a thick neck. Like Santo, he appears to not have an ounce of extra weight on him. He has fine brown hair which he has not combed.

Santo sits next to him and Gaspare sits across from Santo, both just about in front of their respective bunks. Tony sits in the first place on the starboard side at the foot of an empty bunk. Tommy would sit next to Joe Charley and across from Tony, but Tommy rarely comes down from the pilot house for breakfast. Instead, the man on watch makes him a fried-egg sandwich with two eggs. With the sandwich go two oranges and a cup of regular coffee. These are prepared almost immediately and set at the edge of the table where they grow cold while the crew eats. Tommy and food are incidental shipmates.

"Okay, boys, what'll it be? Chiefo, wha'd'ya want this morning?"

Gil is in front of the stove, the frying pan, now empty of the bacon, is spitting grease, and there is a dozen fresh eggs in a carton on the counter. Tony wants fried, two, over. Joe Charley wants three "looking at you." Santo and Gaspare, who have yet to say anything, are still working on their oranges. No one is drinking the grapefruit juice. Gaspare is rejecting one orange after the other, cutting them through once, deciding they are too dried out, and reaching for another. Finally he gives up and takes the least dry one, quarters it, and slurps it off the peel.

"You hungry, Gaspare?" Gil asks. Gaspare nods he is. "Fried?" Gil asks. Gaspare nods and holds up two fingers from the peel he holds pressed to his mouth. "Same for you, Santo?" Santo growls. "Those two can't even pee without the other," Gil thinks to himself, and turns back to the stove.

Tony pours himself a cup of coffee. He is too short to do it sitting down and has to stand at the end of the table, leaning into it for support while he grabs the pot with one hand, the white mug with the other, and slowly pours. The boat pitches forward and Tony follows the pitch with both the cup and the pot, and when the boat heaves back, throwing him backward, he arches himself against the table and keeps pouring. When he's finished he finds Joe Charley's cup waiting, and Santo's, and Gaspare's, and he pours them all while continuing the arabesque. And not a drop spills.

The men eat in silence, yet it is noisy in the forecastle. The roar of the engine, the whirring of the galley fans, the constant cracking of waves against the bow, and the pitching of the boat banging pans and cans and plates together. And the heat in the forecastle together with the smell of bacon fat and coffee and toast and even orange rinds seems to fill the spaces left by the silence of the men. And there is the radio which drones in the background mumbling things about an Israeli attack on a Lebanese outpost and a slowdown on the central artery and the storm off the Carolinas moving up the coast with high winds predicted and three to five inches of snow possible for southern New England.

The crew hears that. Tony surmises it will blow out to sea, but Gil points out that the storms always seem to touch home on the Bay of Fundy. Every year it's the same thing up here, and doesn't Tony remember last year off Brown's Bank they'd had to jog three days because the weather was so bad. They both agree you can't tell, and there's nothing you can do about it anyway.

And Joe Charley, finally full, says the old man's probably getting hungry and he ought to get his breakfast up to him. Then pours himself another cup of coffee, squeezing in close to the table to let Santo get past with his dirty dishes.

Gaspare follows Santo down the other side. In spite of all the bucking and the resulting bad night, Gaspare has eaten a full breakfast, replete with three pieces of toast and four slices of bacon. For there is only one sure antidote to seasickness the fishermen know of, and that is eating. The theory, as they explain it, is that if you are going to be sick, you ought to have something to be sick with, otherwise you dehydrate and that's when seasickness becomes dangerous. The other remedy is working, and that will come soon enough. Gaspare also knows that within a couple of hours the bucking will be over, the boat will have to slow down in order to fish, and his seasickness will vanish for the rest of the trip.

Gaspare and Santo lay their dirty dishes in the sink.

Gaspare looks in the mirror over the sink and runs his fingers through his hair, slicking it back on his head. Tight and wavy, the hair looks perfectly combed. Already a beard is appearing on his cheeks and the boat has only been under way one day. He looks older. The two men then go to the oilskin locker and begin to pull on first the pants, then the jackets. Each wears a heavy wool shirt and Santo has a short-sleeve, white wool sweater over that. They chat together in Italian and Gil, the only Portuguese on board, goes "Mumble, mumble," and the two men stop talking and head up the ladder.

His conscience getting the better of him, Joe Charley dumps his dishes, grabs his parka off Gil's bunk, takes the fried-egg sandwich and the coffee, stuffs the oranges into his pockets, and heads aft to his father in the pilot house.

Tony remains. The breakfast over, Gil makes himself two fried eggs and sits down to what remains on the table: four cold slices of bread, three slices of bacon, the fat congealing on them, no oranges, and a cup and a half of lukewarm coffee. Gil is satisfied.

"What you got to read, Cook?" Tony asks.

"Want one a them of Santo's?" Gil says through a mouthful of toast.

"That shit? No. What d'you got?"

Gil puts his fork down and twists around to look in his bunk. There are two copies of the *Mother Earth News*, *The Gulag Archipelago*, *Bury My Heart at Wounded Knee*, three volumes of *Reader's Digest* condensed novels, and a number of seed and woodworking tools catalogues.

"Just got this in the mail before we left. Here," and he throws a Burpee seed catalogue across the galley table to Tony.

"You get anything done on that little house of yours

outback?" Tony asks, thumbing through the catalogue.

"A little work on the eaves. That fucking brother of yours, he don't stay in long enough to get aything done."

"What are you going to do?" says Tony.

And the two of them chat on while overhead come the sounds of coils of wire being dragged from the bins in the doghouse and across the floor to the deck.

"We'll be setting out pretty soon now, I guess," Tony says.

"Sounds that way," Gil says. Neither man moves.

Once, long ago in Sicily, Tony trained to be a tailor, and two years ago Gil quit fishing to be a carpenter. They understand each other.

"I gotta get up there and do what I gotta do," says Tony.

"Guess I better get these dishes cleaned up before," Gil says.

"See you," Tony says, pulling on his navy jacket. "In the movies."

"Okay, Chiefo . . . and tell your brother to stop talking on the horn. He's going to have the whole fleet up here when he's done."

"Yah, well, what are you going to do? He gets lonely up there."

# 3

---

# *Setting Out*

**"W**hat the fuck're you waiting for? Tie the fucking
thing and get the net overboard."

Tommy's leaning out the open pilot house window, glaring, the microphone for the loudspeaker clutched in his
hand. Impatience is clearly written into his scowl.

On deck below him, five hooded heads look up at him,
then turn back to the work of preparing the net for setting
out. Only on Gil's face is there a trace of a smile. He has
been on boats too long to be ruffled by barks from the pilot
house.

". . . And I mean you, you dumb, fucking Portuguee,"
Tommy shouts.

"Hold your horses, Cap. We're getting there," Gil yells
back, and pulls tight the last slip in the knot tying the end
of the net closed. "Take 'er up, Santo . . ."

The net is about to go overboard for the first time in the
trip. It will go over at least four dozen more times before
the trip is over, five to six times a day for ten to twelve days.
In the thirty-six years Tommy has been fishing he's seen the
net go over more than 45,000 times. And come back sometimes so full the crew could walk on it as it bobbed beside
the boat, and sometimes so ripped up a shark could swim

through it untouched. At one point later in the trip it will come up with only six fish after a three-hour tow.

It's the fisherman's gamble and Tommy loves it. It is what he lives for more than anything else, and for the last twenty hours he has been waiting for the moment to set the nets.

With one eye on the crew below, Tommy continues to check the depthfinder and the fishscope fixed to the starboard wall beside him. They give no sign of fish, but at a certain point Tommy has no choice—the net has to go overboard. He can't keep criss-crossing the grounds until he thinks he has fish below. The market doesn't pay much for fish captains think they've spotted.

"Higher, Santo . . . up . . . higher."

Joe Charley is swinging his hand around over his head and Santo is wrapping the line from the long gilson around the revolving niggerhead at the far end of the winch. The gilson is fixed to the roller cable and the rollers are slowly rising from their place along the starboard gunwales until they are about level with the rail.

"Hold it . . . hold it," both Gil and Joe Charley yell above the roar of the diesel winch engine. The rollers sway in the wind and the boat, now still in the water, is bounced sideways from a wave breaking on her side and the spray leaps over the rail and into the faces of Gil, Joe Charley, and Tony as they stand behind the rollers, rocking them back and forth, creating momentum until, at that certain point, Joe Charley yells, "Slack it," and Santo quickly releases the gilson and the three men cry "Heyyy!" in unison and rush forward like linemen on a blocking dummy, and over the rail go some of the rollers, pulling the chain after them, and with the chain more rollers; and the crew grabs at recalcitrant rollers and heave these after the others; and the roller and the chain fall down along the side of the boat, and the net begins to follow after; and the crew scoops up armfuls of net and heave them after, carefully watching they don't become caught up themselves and pulled overboard . . . until only the cod end with the slip knot Tommy was yelling about remains; and that, too, is picked up by the gilson and shoved overboard just as the rollers were . . . and suddenly the deck is empty again, except for a few dried fish that had not been cleaned out of the net when it was stored away at the end of the last trip. These are kicked down the deck toward the scuppers and a wave breaking against the boat washes through the scuppers and carries them out to sea.

The deck is clear. The net is in the water. The crew watches it sink. Tommy watches the crew on deck. They signal that the net is partially under the boat and could foul the "wheel" or the propellor if the boat begins to move forward.

Carefully, Tommy sets the boat in reverse, pushes the rudder to port, then gives a quick burst of speed to the propellor and puts the engine out of gear and waits. The thrust of the propellor should at once drive the net from beneath the boat while moving the stern away from the net. He repeats the process and Gaspare looks up and nods. The net is free.

Tommy starts the boat forward with a slight turn to starboard, leaving the net just aft of amidships. Santo and Gaspare take their places at the winch, Santo handling the forward wire, Gaspare the after wire. Gil goes to the forward gallows, Tony to the after gallows. Joe Charley remains along the rail, standing by to help.

Slowly the large winch drums begin to unwind and the two wires to the net inch up the deck, around the deck bollards, one to the forward gallows, the other back down along the gunwales to the after gallows. At this point everything is slow and easy and the men are tense and quiet at their posts.

"Hold it like that," Gil yells to Santo and the forward wire stops while Gil makes it fast to the forward door. He has to reach inside the frame. The door is banging on the side of the boat and the boat rides crossways to the wind. He does his work quickly and gets away from the door.

"Yah. Okay," he yells.

"Wait a minute," Tony calls. He and Gaspare are making the after door fast.

"Let 'er go," Tony says.

Gaspare and Santo look up at Tommy in the pilot house window. Tommy nods, reaches for the throttle, and puts the engine at three-quarter speed, holding the course in a wide arc to starboard.

Santo and Gaspare release the brakes on the two winch drums and the wires begin to whip off the winch, racing up the length of the deck, around the bollards, across the deck and back along the gunwale, through the gallows bollard set in the peak of the A-frame, and down into the water after the disappearing net. Two hundred fifty fathoms—1,500 feet—of wire headed diagonally for the bottom.

Gil stands back away, in the door to the doghouse; Tony backs up against the pilot house. Joe Charley joins him. No one wants to be near the wires as they go out. For there is no sudden stopping of the wires.

The big boat shakes, it rattles, it twists and turns as it cuts its course around through the sea and bites into waves, sending them streaming over the bow in blankets of spray the length of the deck and up against the pilot house and into the cold, serious faces of Santo and Gaspare, who stare at the outgoing wires, counting the twenty-five-fathom marks. Gaspare reaches behind him and pulls on a little bell. It tinkles incongruously against the roar of the engines and the smacking of the waves. Tommy slows the boat to a crawl, and Santo and Gaspare ease on the brake drums. The boat settles down to a gentle heaving. The wires are paid out gradually until they are even, the fathom marks in line.

The first tow of the trip is under way. The crew heads forward for a mug of coffee. They are quiet and finish their coffee quickly. Joe Charley gets up from the galley table, washes out his mug, sets it in the rack in front of the stove, and announces he's "going back aft and dream about what I'd be doing if I was home now."

Santo climbs into his bunk, takes out one of his issues of *Stop* and resumes his ongoing studies. Gaspare puts on a heavy army-surplus jacket and a brown fishing cap and heads aft to the pilot house with a cup of coffee for Tommy. Gil pulls out a tool catalogue, sits at the galley table, and starts thumbing through it, while Tony sits opposite him, leaning on his elbows, his mug of coffee still half-full in front of him, and absently listens to the music on the radio. He gets up, pours out the remainder of the coffee into the sink, washes out the cup, puts it on the rack, pulls on his aviator cap, shrugs into his coat, and without a word climbs the ladder and follows Gaspare and Joe Charley aft.

It is 9:30 on a Sunday morning. One hundred eighty miles to the southward their wives and families are preparing to go to Mass or are returning. And the storm that was building off the Carolinas has just dropped four inches of snow on New York City.

# 4

## On the Tow

Tommy's eating another orange. It's his second in the past ten minutes and there are rinds scattered all over the near end of the shelf that runs between the two stools across the front of the pilot house. And there are rinds in the empty styrofoam coffee cup on the window sill in front of him.

He pulls the window open in front of him and heaves the cup out toward the deck. The wind sweeps it away, but some of the rinds fall to the deck below, almost hitting Joe Charley as he makes his way aft.

"Pick 'em up!" Tommy yells down.

"Okay, Cap. Anything you say, Cap," and he bends down, flings the rinds sideways over the rail, and continues making his way aft to his bunk by the engine room.

Tommy pulls the window back up, picks up the last orange . . . and puts it back down. And looks at the depthfinder beside him.

"Five degrees to port," he says, and Gaspare, sitting in the port stool, elbows on the window sill, gazing silently out at the gray sea running across the bows, leans down and turns the dial on the automatic pilot which is fixed to the forward wall under the shelf.

"Hold it there," Tommy says, picks up the orange again

and sets it down again, and gets off his stool and walks to the starboard door in the rear corner of the pilot house, steps outside and, holding the door open, takes a leak down the iron ladder leading to the deck. And checks the wires to the net as they cut together through the water, and steps back inside, slamming the door behind him.

"Bring it back again," Tommy says, and as Gaspare reaches down for the automatic pilot, Tommy walks into the chart room . . . and descends the short ladder into his stateroom. From a rack by the head of his rumpled bunk he pulls a pack of cigarettes which he jams into the breast pocket of his checked wool shirt.

Mounting the ladder, he stops in the chart room and looks over a rack of record tapes which he studies carefully. The rack stretches the width of the chart room and is full of tapes. He chooses one, slips the tape out of its box, and turning around sticks it into a tape deck fixed onto the wall dividing the chart room from the pilot house.

And suddenly the place is filled with the opening strains of *La Traviata* blaring from the speakers stuck into the opposite corners of the pilot house.

Gaspare looks up at the speaker over his head, imperceptibly shrugs his shoulders, and returns to staring out the window.

And Tommy goes back to his stool, pulls the fresh pack out of his pocket, rips the cellophane off, grabs at a cigarette, finds a match on the shelf, and lights up. And immediately looks over at Gaspare.

"What the fuck're you staring at?" he demands of Gaspare, who is watching Tommy out of the corner of his eye. "What do I care, you don't smoke? You don't want smoke, stand outside."

It's true, Gaspare doesn't like the smoke, and it's

equally true that Tommy doesn't care. But that's not the issue. Tommy had told everybody he was going to stop smoking this trip, and had even brought along a supply of lifesavers to help him—and a couple of cartons of cigarettes, just in case. Gaspar has seen Tommy try before, but he's never seen him fail so quickly. Even Tommy's a little surprised at himself, and as he relaxes back into his swivel stool he is already promising himself that the next time he just won't tell anybody.

"You're a little old lady," Tommy says.

Gaspare shakes his head. He can't hear Tommy because the music is blaring so.

"You're an *old lady,*" Tommy yells. This time Gaspare nods he's heard, and smiles and goes back to staring out the window.

For seven years Gaspare has fished with Tommy and for seven years he's watched Tommy give up cigarettes, and he's heard himself called an "old lady" and been told he runs his household like a concentration camp; and he's learned not to argue with the captain.

He can see Tommy is poised, waiting for an argument. Not only does he have his cigarettes back but the music is on, and once the music is playing in the pilot house Tommy is fortified. No one on board has the voice or the stamina to compete with practically the full index of Italian operas turned on at nearly full volume, a throbbing 600-horsepower engine below, and a captain who has assumed the prerogative of being right ninety-nine percent of the time and not wrong the rest. And, like the others of the crew, Gaspare acquiesces to Tommy, not because he is scared of him or because Tommy is right, but because Tommy is the captain.

On a good fishing boat, the distance between the

forecastle and the pilot house is far greater than the fifty or so feet that separate the two. The crew lives in the forecastle, the captain in the pilot house, and only rarely does a good captain allow himself to be a part of the crew, and almost never while the boat is fishing.

He keeps to himself. He will come forward for meals, but usually eats quickly and returns to quarters. And when he is forward, the crew is seldom itself. If they are relaxed, they are subdued when he is there. They may call him "Cap" and they may make a joke softly at his expense, but they rarely talk about fishing with him—or he with them. They never ask when the boat is heading in or where it will move to or if it is going to move at all. They will certainly never to his face suggest that there has been a lot of damage recently and why doesn't he find better bottom to work (although after he's gone the griping may be vicious).

And when he enters a discussion and offers a contrary opinion, they might disagree, but only say, "Well, I don't know, Cap, that may be." They'd never say, "Cap, you're full of shit" or "You don't know what the fuck you're talking about."

And these may be men who have fished with him for years. They may even be family or *compares,* and their wives may be best friends or sisters. They may be better educated. They may be former captains themselves. But as long as the boat is out, the captain's word is law as clearly and resoundingly and certainly as infallibly as the pope's.

"North-by-east," Tommy says, his voice modulated exactly to reach Gaspare through the roar in the pilot house.

Tommy is no longer paying attention to Gaspare. Instead, he is concentrating on the depthfinder at his side and the fishscope beneath it, watching not just for the proper depths, but for fish. Specks beside the heavy line might be fish. They might also be feed or just ricochets off the bottom. If there are fish, the bleeping light on the opaque screen of the fishscope will flatten out horizontally.

Knowing that there are fish below is reassuring, but it doesn't help catch them on the immediate tow. However, when Tommy sees there are fish, he quickly takes a bearing on the Loran and scribbles it down on a piece of scrap paper lying among the ashes, matches, old copies of *Fishermen's International* or the *National Fisherman* on the shelf. Later, when the net is hauled back and he sees it is full of haddock or cod, he recalls what the fishscope told him earlier. If the net is filled with redfish or pollock or hake, he may disregard the information, but at least he knows where the fish are—exactly—and he can always go back for them.

And that's why Tommy rarely sleeps while the boat is towing, which can mean he will be prowling the pilot house for days on end, rarely strolling too far from his corner. He explains it this way:

"On the Italian planes during the war they had written on the noses: 'If you don't trust yourself, don't expect me to do it for you.' That means, you gotta pay attention, you gotta do the work. Isn't nobody going to do it for you. I always say, any captain who sleeps and lets someone else fish, he gonna catch no fish. You see, it's these little things no one's gonna remember. They don't think about it. They forget. You gotta do the thinking. You gotta remember."

And that's why Tommy is trying to provoke Gaspare into an argument. It keeps him awake, gives him something to do.

"You don't look no good, Gaspare. You sick last night?"

Gaspare lifts his hand a few inches off the window sill, tilts it back and forth a couple of times—*metza, metza*—and smiles.

"Better'n being home with those two wives of yours." (Gaspare's mother-in-law lives with him.)

Gaspare leans closer toward the window. He can feel Tommy's needle headed for him. Two more questions and Tommy will accuse him of running a concentration camp at home.

"Yah, two, three days home, that's enough, isn't it? Then you get out here, don't have to worry about nothing. Sleep, eat, take it easy. No kids yelling, waking you up."

Tommy is leaning back in his stool. He's swiveled it around so that he's facing Gaspare. Only the twitching at the corners of his squinting eyes disturbs the deadpan look on his face.

Gaspare looks over at him. There's something in his blood that tugs at him to defend his household. Then he shrugs and glances up at the clock behind him. It's 10:35 A.M. Another hour and a half before hauling back.

"I know," Tommy says. "I couldn't live in a concentration camp like that. You know, one of these days those kids of yours are going to say, 'I'll see you later,' and . . ."

And Gaspare raises his hand.

"All I know is, I do the best I can. We'll see what happens," Gaspare says.

And Tommy smiles.

"Northeast, Gaspare."

# 5

---

# *Hauling Back*

**O**n deck it's cold, although the film of ice has vanished with the dawn. It may be thirty-five degrees, but the wind is holding steady at 15 miles per hour and the seas have only barely diminished. And while the boat has slowed to a trawl and no longer plunges, but rolls through the swells, an occasional wave cracks off the bow and pours down off the doghouse onto the main deck or streams in through the scuppers and sloshes under and around the checkerboards laid out to form pens on the asphalt-tiled deck and runs back out the scuppers.

And overhead the thick gray sky threatens snow, and low over the water clouds of vapor still form here and there; and with the exception of a bobbing gull or a Mother Carey chicken dashing over the cresting waves, there is nothing in sight except the *Joseph & Lucia III* and the unending blue-gray ocean.

And as Tommy and Gaspare hold down the watch, Joe Charley is stretched out on his bunk in the afterquarters, curled up on his side under a brown blanket, his shut eyes faced toward the port hull where a color photograph of his one-year-old daughter Nicole, dressed in baby-blue, is taped. Across the cramped quarters, Tony lies propped up by his pillow, his glasses on, reading *The Chariot of the Gods.* A small radio at the foot of his bed is barely audible in the pounding roar that rises through the open door leading to the engine room. There is a pervasive smell of fuel oil mixed in hot air.

Tony looks at his watch, puts the book down on the shelf beside him, and, without bothering to flick off the soft reading light over his head, slides down the pillow and falls asleep.

Forward, Gil sits at the end of the bench by his bunk, a white plastic garbage pail at his feet, peeling potatoes. He has stripped down to his undershirt and his brow is beaded with drops of sweat. The fan over the stove tugs at the heat of the galley, while below it on the stove a pot of water comes to a boil and in the oven chicken fries.

And by the sink the radio blares, checked only by the steady drone of the engine, fifty feet, an empty hold, and two thick steel bulkheads away, and by the roar of the fan and the shivers of the boat laboring into the seas hauling the net 1,000 feet below; and the pots and pans in the cupboards vibrate against each other, setting up a muffled din.

And Gil hums to himself off-key and tosses a peeled potato into a pot on the galley table, picks up another potato from the pile lying on his bunk, and wipes the sweat off his brow with the back of the hand which holds the knife.

And Santo lies asleep in his bunk, flat on his back, rigid, his arms at his side, his face turned up into the reading light which is on, a copy of *Stop* folded over his chest. His mouth is open.

And there is a blast from the foghorn!

Gil cranes his neck to look past the ladder at the galley clock.

"Hauling back, Santo," Gil says, and rises, wiping peelings from his lap and lifting the cover off the bench and taking out two cans of beets and two more cans of cut beans, and, cradling them and kicking the garbage pail aside, walks to the counter and drops them.

Santo practically bounds from his bed, not from enthusiasm, but from having been propelled by the foghorn out of a sound sleep into a world he had momentarily forgotten. Once awake and familiar with his whereabouts, he relaxes back into himself, the slow, deliberate, almost-mechanical workman.

He shoves himself off the edge of his bunk onto the bench and tightropes along it around the galley table, holding onto the line of bunks until he reaches the floor. He is pulling on a heavy sweater when Gaspare clumps down the ladder. He mumbles something to Santo, who smiles slightly, then both go to the locker and pull out their oilskins which are still damp from setting out the net three hours before.

There seems to be no rush. Santo and Gaspare dress slowly. Gil pours the peeled potatoes into the boiling water, checks the frying chicken, then begins to open the cans of beets and beans. Joe Charley plunges down the stairs and makes immediately for the far corner by the stove and grabs a handful of cookies, and, with his mouth half full and one hand on a coffee cup, says, "Hauling back, boys. Let's go. The Old Man's wondering where everyone is."

"Go fry your ass," Gil says.

"Nice talk, Cook," Joe Charley answers, pouring out half a cup of coffee.

Without saying a word, first Gaspare, then Santo, starts up the ladder to the deck.

"Let's go," Santo states.

"Fucking greasers," Joe Charley says, but not before assuring himself Gaspare and Santo have passed onto the deck.

* * *

Gil sits in the doorway of the doghouse, elbows resting on knees, chin in hands, staring at the wire being reeled slowly out of the water, up through the gallows across and down the middle of the deck to the huge, sea-rusted winch behind which Gaspare and Santo stand, their hands gripped on the separate brake drum wheels. The wires, stretched taut by the heavy drag of the net being pulled up from the bottom, shiver, sending thin sheets of water onto the deck, laying a line of wetness directly beneath their course.

Joe Charley and Tony stand together by the door of the whaleback, leaning against the side of the pilot house behind which the auxillary engine for the winch roars deafeningly. They don't try to talk and instead stare out at the sea running off from the boat and the cloud of black smoke blowing from the stack above them.

Tommy leans out the window of the pilot house, his arms crossed on the sill, his chin resting on his arms. He stares at the starboard rail. He's cold and serious. He alone senses the moment of anticipation: Are there fish in the net, and if there are, what kind and how many? This first set may well set the tenor of the trip. He's come to Grand Manan Banks for gray sole. This was his gamble. If there are no gray sole, what is there? pollock (there's no price on

pollock)? cod (at thirty cents a pound there'll have to be
a lot of them)? hake (the price has been rising but it's still
not near cod, but it's better than pollock; still, it's hard to
find enough hake to make a trip)? cusk (no way—the price
is all right, but there are just not enough cusk)? redfish
(good for filling out a percentage if there are enough haddock caught, but you have to catch too many redfish to
make a trip and they take up too much space unless that's
all there is)? haddock (good price, big demand at the mar-
ketplace, but the quota only allows two thousand pounds,
or ten percent of the total catch, so if the boat has set on
a school of haddock, then it's good to have redfish on
board)?

It seems endless. The hauling back. The thousand feet
of wire which ran out with such a rush when the net was
set returns laboriously, foot by foot, with a strain that
makes the boat quiver and heel over.

Almost imperceptibly, the wires which had stretched
out nearly horizontally along the side of the boat cut more
acutely down into the water until at last they are pulling
straight down, heeling the boat hard to starboard, telling
the men the net is now rising off the bottom.

Gil stands up, moves to the rail, and casually leans
against it, watching for the tip of the door to break the
surface.

Joe Charley pushes himself off the pilot house wall, goes
inside the whaleback, and emerges with a pair of orange
rubber gloves which he pulls on as he makes his way to the
rail amidships.

Tony steps to the after gallows and lifts the iron hook
from its place on the frame and continues to stare out to
sea.

Gaspare and Santo tighten up a twist on the brake drum

and they turn their eyes toward Joe Charley who is leaning over the rail looking down, his right arm extended upward.

And suddenly the forward door appears at the edge of the rail, and Gil, hook in hand, poised, his feet spread solidly beneath him, yells "Hold it," and as the thousand-pound door strikes the steel gallows, he aims and tosses the hook through the bracket on the door, quickly reaches in and pulls back on the chain attached to the hook. Santo backs off the drum and the wire slips back down the gallows, the door toward the water—and stops, held fast by the hook, then slams into the side of the boat. And Gil jumps back and waits for the door to swing out again, quickly frees the wire from the door, and pulls away, yelling "Take it up," and Santo puts the winch in gear again and the reeling in continues until the tip of the net breaks water and climbs toward the gallows, and Santo tightens down the brake altogether and waits for Gaspare and Tony to make the after wire fast.

Off the side, about twenty feet out from the boat, the end of the net pops to the surface, like a submerged balloon, buoyed by the fish within.

Tommy stares at it. He sees silver and black and a little green, with speckles of red here and there.

It is still hard to tell what is there, but Tommy can see that whatever it is, it isn't much. He calculates. He knows the line he has just towed and he figures that to retow it would be to repeat the catch. He goes to the chart room, getting his Loran reading on the way. He locates himself and decides to change course and try more to the northeast.

By the time he returns to his place by the window, the net is swinging across the deck, Gil and Joe Charley chasing after the line beneath it. As it comes to a stop over the port pen, Gil and Joe Charley yank at the line and the bottom of the net opens and the fish stream over the deck.

"Pollock," Tommy mumbles to himself, "and a little cod, some haddock," and shakes his head in disgust. There may be gray sole in there somewhere, but there are none on the top of the pile, which has to mean there isn't much around. They're somewhere else. The "big killing" gamble has to be scratched. Now the question is, what else is there?

Tommy reaches up and grabs the loudspeaker microphone.

"Hurry it up! Let's get that fucking thing back over," and hangs the microphone back up and reaches for the Citizen's Band phone overhead.

"Hey, Nino," he calls to his brother 180 miles to the southward, "Come in, Nino . . ."

* * *

In the middle of the deck just forward of the winch is a large, welded steel vat. It sits exactly between the two metal hatch covers leading into the hold. And from one end of the vat leads a chute made up of rollers. The chute stops just before the after hatch. And there is a hose attached to the top of the vat and to a tap below the front of the winch. Santo tightens down the brake drum, coils the line for the long gilson, hanging it on the winch, and, coming from behind the winch, turns on the tap and the vat begins to fill with swishing water.

The area between the vat and the port rail is penned off with checkerboards. The largest pen is forward and is filled with the fish from the tow.

And forward of the large pen sits a bollard and on top

of the bollard is a small wooden box filled with twine and needles for mending the nets and knives for cleaning the fish.

Even as the net is still going out, Gil has moved to the box, taken one of the knives, and from a slot along the bollard has drawn a long, round steel and is sharpening the knife. He is joined by Tony, who rummages through the box to find his own knife, tests the edge and waits for Gil to finish, then takes a few strokes on the steel. As the boat slows to a trawl and the wires are made fast, the two men step over the checkerboard into the pile of fish. Some are squirming, others flapping, more are still.

They work their feet into the pile until they have footing on the deck below, their legs spread and solid, then each grabs a large pollock by the nose, flips it over on its back, and with one motion slits across the gills so the head breaks backward, then slits down from the breastbone to the tail. The entrails bulge out. They heave the fish into the pen by the large steel vat where the fish wriggle about for a few seconds and expire with their cold yellow eyes staring blankly to the side.

Joe Charley and Santo seat themselves on the edge of a checkerboard, their feet stretched out among the dead fish. Over the edge of the checkerboard they have placed sections of an old tire for a cushion. They reach down, grab a fish by holding one side of the broken breastbone, flip it across their knees, and, keeping a firm grasp with their left hand, rip out the entrails with their right, throwing the entrails into the pen behind them, then heaving the fish up and over the edge of the vat in which the water is swirling.

They work silently, only barely able to keep up with the fish being tossed into the pen at their feet. It takes only a few fish before the fronts of their oilskins run red with blood, and flakes of blood and gurry speckle their faces and stick to their pants. Behind them a pile of entrails grows, and soon their feet are buried in cod, haddock, pollock, hake, cusk; and even in the cold, damp air sweat breaks out and runs down their faces and into their eyes, and they wipe it out with the backs of their gloves. And once in awhile a wave breaks over the rail and washes down over them.

And cutting into the roar of the engine and the sloshing of the fish washing down over the rollers into the hold and the water running through the scuppers and around the deck comes the oozing, suffering strains of broken-hearted lovers replete with mandolins, compliments of Tommy and his tapes. And Gil looks up at the cross trees on the mast where a loudspeaker is fixed, and, a cod in one hand, a bloody knife in the other, sighs, and heaves the cod into the pen.

And Tony begins to sing to himself . . .

* * *

Gaspare is in the hold. It is freezing down there, but he is already perspiring and has taken off his yellow oilskin jacket as he chips at the pile of crushed ice amidships. With a heavy bar he whacks at it, breaking off pieces and chunks, then throws the bar down and picks up a three-pronged pitchfork and stabs at the fish that are sliding down the chute through the hatch and dropping fifteen feet to the corrugated steel floor—cod, haddock, pollock, all in a mix in a pile at his feet and the pile growing too fast—and he flings the cod to the stainless-steel pen in the far corner, the pollock to the pen behind him, the haddock to the pen in the near corner. Then he drops the pitchfork and takes up a shovel and covers the fish with a layer of ice.

But even as he maintains his frantic pace, he is careful

to lay the fish flat and side by side, knowing that the two thousand pounds from the first set may swell to seventy thousand by the end of the trip, and there has to be room if that happens.

It is the kind of work for which Gaspare is geared. It requires a sense of order, of meticulousness coupled with a feeling for proportion. Without knowing, Gaspare has to know that the haddock from the first set will or will not hold constant and that he will need two pens, not just one for the trip, that there will be more or less pollock this trip and set aside enough room at the beginning so that ten days later he is not mixing fish.

For later the fish all have to come out and be delivered to the buyers in Boston, and there will be a number of buyers, some wanting only cod, others only gray sole, others wanting cod and haddock but no pollock, others pollock and lemon sole. It will be a rush when the fish are taken out. Instead of Gaspare in the hold there will be lumpers, or stevedores, who will not know which fish are where, and on shore there will be lumpers dumping the fish into carts and they will not want half a cart of pollock and the other half redfish, nor will they want a cart mixed with large cod, market cod, and scrod cod. They'll want all of one, then all of the other, and they'll raise hell if the fish come out of the hold helter-skelter.

But even more important, before the fish are even taken out they will have to be auctioned at market and Tommy will want to know how many pounds of each species and gradations within the species there are below. And only Gaspare will know—within a hundred or two hundred pounds. He knows how much fish one pen can hold if they are packed correctly and iced just right. Too few fish in a layer means more ice is necessary to cover them. Too much ice cuts down on the number of pounds of fish, for the buyers automatically take off a percentage for the ice. But too little ice will not hold the fish properly and the flesh will begin to deteriorate; and while the cod may have been clean, free of worms, the flesh strong when it was caught, ten days later it may be spoiled—and the top price goes to the number one fish. If the buyer feels the fish is not number one, he'll call for a resale, claiming he's getting number two fish and the thirty-five cents a pound the boat might have received may be cut in half, and a good trip can be diminished by a half and the long days away from home can become—like that—a waste of time.

Gaspare works on in silence, whittling away at the pile of fish beside him, only half-aware that fewer and fewer fish are falling through the hatch.

"That's it," he hears from above.

"What's that?" he yells, looking up at the open hatch. Santo is looking down.

"That's it, goumba."

Gaspare nods and goes back to work separating the fish and putting on the final layer of crushed ice.

* * *

The last fish has been swished from the vat and Gil has already gone below to the galley to put lunch on the table.

Santo goes aft to the base of the pilot house and picks up a hose which lies there pumping water along the deck and out the scuppers. He hauls it forward and drops it over a checkerboard for Tony, who begins to wash down the pen he and Gil had been working in.

The tops of some of the checkerboards are wet with blood. Scales stick on the sides and to the deck, which is slippery from the slime of the fish.

He hoses everything down carefully, washing small her-ring and sea urchins and seaweed out of the corners and from under the boards, then starts on the pile of entrails, filling that pen with water, forming a foul, pinkish pool in which the entrails float.

Joe Charley lifts one of the checkerboards and the water rushes aft, floating the entrails with it. He lifts a second board and the water runs free on the deck, and, as the boat rolls from side to side, the water and its cargo flows back and forth across the deck and alternately out the port and starboard scuppers.

The deck cleared and washed down, Tony turns the hose on Joe Charley, who stands stock still, hands down at his side, facing him. Gently, holding the hose up and angling it down, he lets the water run first across the front of the jacket, then along the arms. Joe Charley turns around and Tony washes down his back. While he's doing the back, Joe Charley scrubs his front with his gloves, breaking loose any stuck particles, then he leans over and scrubs his pant legs, front and back. He again faces Tony who gives him one more washing over and hands the hose to Joe Charley, who in turn washes him down. Santo has gone to a second hose hanging along the pilot house and has done the whole job himself. Each man takes off his rubber gloves and imerses them in the water, rings them out, and then heads to his quarters, Tony and Joe Charley aft, Santo forward.

Only Gaspare remains on deck, that is, below decks, icing down the remaining fish.

And over the vacated deck the DiMara sisters are carry-ing on in close two-part harmony.

* * *

Throughout, Tommy has been sitting at the pilot house window, talking with his brother Nino on the *Joseph & Lucia II.*

Nino's working Jeffreys Ledge forty miles to the north of Gloucester, and he's set on cod. Tommy tells him he's got maybe six hundred pounds haddock, a thousand pounds pollock, but two baskets of gray sole, and he doesn't know what he'll do. Try a few more tows, see what's around.

It's a brotherly chat—or seems to be. The two seem to be just talking, passing the time, but each knows that they can be—and undoubtedly are being—listened to by other boats. And that's all right, but the brothers aren't about to give any real information away, so couched in their desultory tone are messages, plans, advice which only the two of them understand, a language that has taken years of fishing to build up.

And all the time the music has been on full in the pilot house. And now that he and Nino are no longer talking, Tommy is singing along with the DiMara sisters while his eyes move between the depthfinder and the fishscope.

Tommy likes the DiMara sisters. Not only do they "sing good in Italian, they sing good in English." And they make a lot of money and their mother is American, and somehow it all fits. They have satisfied certain criteria and thereby earned the right to fish with him. And they sound only vaguely seasick.

Joe Charley comes up to the pilot house through his father's cabin. He is still drying his hands on his pants.

"O.K. Cap," he says, "why don't you go forward and get something to eat."

"Shoal water's to port," Tommy says.

"That's good, Cap."

"Hold it at a hundred and ten,"

"O.K., Cap. Got it. Go eat."

And no sooner has Tommy put on his red cap and descended the starboard ladder to the deck than Joe Charley switches off the DiMara sisters, not only from the deck and the pilot house, but has removed them from the tape deck altogther and Lynn Anderson takes their place. Joe Charley and his father do not hold the same criteria.

# 6

---

# *Getting the Trip*

"**L**ook at all those white bellies. What shame! What a goddamned shame!"

Tommy is frustrated. Ten sets and nothing but haddock. It's pitch-black out. There isn't a star in the sky. The sea is running heavy and the wind is rising from the northwest. The storm that was building Saturday off the Carolinas has moved up the coast. Four inches of snow on New York City, three inches on Boston. It's hugging the shore and not blowing out to sea, which means it should hit Grand Manan Banks anytime—and nothing but haddock.

The boat is shaking, with the winch straining against the sea hauling the net back, and the waves are breaking over the rails and washing down the men and the decks. And while it is not cold enough to freeze hard, the decks are becoming slippery and the men standing open to the weather are cold.

The deck is brightly lighted by the spots fixed to the pilot house and the mast, and the light spreads off the rails onto the running sea to a point just past the hump of the cod end as it bobs in the water. And the gulls swooping in from the black night seem stark white in flight against the backdrop. But it's the white bellies of the haddock pressed together in the net that has caught and held Tommy's eye. For a quick moment he is almost a bitter man.

"You know, the only guys who succeed in this business are the guys that take the chances. Look at all that fucking haddock. What the fuck am I supposed to do with it? All those fucking experts and scientists and know-it-alls, they tell me, 'You can't fish for haddock because there's no haddock out here anymore.' If there's no haddock, what the fuck do you call that? I can't catch nothing else. What am I supposed to do, throw 'em back? That's what I'm supposed to do. That's what all the experts say I got to do. You know what happens I throw 'em back? The gulls'll eat 'em 'cause the fish are dead.

"You know how much money there is there? You know what they're paying for haddock? Sixty-five cents a pound, seventy cents. It's been up to eighty cents. For haddock. And I got to throw 'em back or I get a big fine.

"If I had any guts you know what I'd do? I'd take 'em all, every one I could get, and I'd bring 'em in and I'd land the fuckers, and if those bastards want to fine me, they can have 'em. What are they going to fine me for, for making a living? What am I supposed to do? I can't catch nothing else. But no, they'd fine me, maybe they'd try to take away my license, and they'd take the fish and sell them themselves. And I'll be fucked if I'm going to pay those bastards anything so's they'll look the other way.

"So I gotta stop fishing here. I gotta take those fish on board and I'm going to have too many. I don't know what I'll do with 'em. What a goddamned shame!"

Tommy reaches behind him for the deck microphone.

"Put the net on board. We'll lay to for awhile. See what this weather's going to do."

He gets off his stool and walks back into the chart room,

picking up his Loran bearings on the way. The chart room is dark. He flicks on the small lamp over the chart table, finds the Loran lines he's looking for, reaches for the divider hung in a small holder with a number of pens and pencils on the side wall, makes a dot where the boat is presently, finds Northeast Banks, sets the dividers on the chart—one point on the dot, the other somewhere off Southwest Banks—moves the dividers to the scale at the edge of the chart and calculates the distance between the two points, puts the dividers back in their holder, flicks off the light, and returns to his stool, stopping along the way to put on another tape.

"Fuck it," he says. "We'll see if there are any redfish around."

*  *  *

"It's countdown time," says Joe Charley, leaning into the galley table, cradling a cup of coffee. At his elbows are three milk cookies.

"Bull shit! He ain't got a trip yet," says Gil from his bunk behind Joe Charley. "Shit," Gil says again, only this time he isn't thinking about the trip. The boat has come down hard on a wave and has bounced him off his pillow which would probably have passed unnoticed if he weren't trying to read *The Gulag Archipelago*.

"It's supposed to come sixty from the sou'west," says Tony, who is calmly leaning back against the bunk, a peeled orange in front of him. He states it matter of factly.

"Where the Christ does that man think he is?" says Gil, rolling out of his bunk. He lunges against the pitching boat and reaches for the telephone. Bracing himself, he rings once.

"Hey, Cap, will you turn that fucking stuff off? We're

trying to sleep down here. Yeah! O.K." Gil lurches back to his bunk and crawls in again. "Where does he think he is —in Sicily? In the middle of the goddamned Atlantic in a storm, and we got to listen to that shit at three in the morning."

Suddenly the deck is quiet. The incongruous fiesta going on outside melts away to the pilot house and there is an overwhelming silence in the forecastle.

"They're all going in now, I'll tell you," says Tony, standing up and throwing the orange peels into the garbage can at the foot of the table.

"The other boats going in?" Gil asks from his bunk.

"Yeah," Joe Charley answers. "What do they want to stay out in this shit for?"

"Nino was even talking about going in. Said the *Santa Maria* went in this morning. Said the weather report called for three-, four-day gales," says Gaspare. Gaspare is in his bunk, stretched out, his hands cupped under his head. The color has returned to his face with the fishing, but now that the boat is again jogging the bucking into the seas, he is not feeling himself, and every so often takes a furtive gulp of air and closes his eyes.

"But we're staying out?" Gil asks disgustedly.

"Yeah. The tough stay out, then they go in, and the really tough stay out a little longer," Tony says with a faint smile.

"Where we going?" Gaspare asks.

"Northeast Banks. He's looking for redfish to cover the haddock," Joe Charley answers.

"Goddamn it! Why can't he slow down?" Gil groans, then swings out of his bunk to a place beside Joe Charley. He lays *The Gulag Archipelago* down on the table in front of him.

"What's that about?" Joe Charley asks.

"It's this book about Russia. Jesus, depressing! I almost don't want to read it. How the fuck you supposed to live in a country like that? They murder everyone, people that don't have anything to do with nothing, they murder 'em. What they want to do that for, I don't know. It don't make much sense to me."

"Let me see that," Tony asks.

Gil slides the book across the table to him. Tony picks it up and reads the back cover, thumbs through a few pages in the middle, then slides it back to Gil.

"Let me have it when you're done," he says.

"I don't know what you guys are talking about, but I'm going back for a kink," Joe Charley says and starts to pick up his cup and slide toward the galley. Gil slides with him and moves back to let him out.

"I'll be going, too," says Tony. He stands up, crumbs the table with his hand, then grabs his aviators gap, pulls it on, slips on his jacket, and follows Joe Charley up the ladder.

"Get that lightswitch while you're there, will ya, Chiefo?" Gil calls out. Tony backs down the stairs and reaches out toward one of the support columns on which is fixed a switch box. He flicks it and the lights over the galley table go out. Except for a small bulb hanging by the ship's phone, the forecastle is dark. Gil crawls back into his bunk. Gaspare hauls his blanket up around his neck and closes his eyes.

And the boat slows down. The bucking stops. The boat rolls slowly and the only sound is the soft clunk of *The Gulag Archepelago* landing on the shelf beside Gil's bunk.

And then the big engine aft begins to turn over again

and the boat goes back to pounding its way through the coming seas, and Gil mumbles "Shit," and closes his eyes.

And in the pilot house Santo sits alone in the captain's swivel stool, leaning on his elbows, staring out the window. All the lights are out. The green numbers flicker on the Loran C. On the two Loran Bs the white lines race each other across the screen. Santo yawns, looks up at the clock, accepts that he has half an hour to go on his watch, and goes back to staring out at the black sea. A wave washes over the bows and smacks on the pilot house and races down over the windows. Santo doesn't blink. A half an hour to go.

And for the first time in two days Tommy is wrapped up in his blanket on his bunk. Asleep.

\* \* \*

"Dogfish, Cap."

The net has just popped up off the starboard. It is speckled with red and grey. It's a full bag but it isn't bright red, which means there's a lot of dogfish and dogfish are the nemesis of the fishermen. They are no good for anything except for throwing overboard, and while they are in the net they destroy the fish around them.

"Goddamn. Stupid. I am stupid. I'm not thinking good," says Tommy aloud to no one. "Store the net. We're steaming," he yells down to the deck.

Once again he goes to the chart room and plots his course to the southwest, 150 miles to Jeffreys Ledge, or forty miles from Gloucester.

He returns to his stool, turns off the depthfinder and the fishscope, waits for the net to be brought on board and the catch to be dropped on the deck, then he eases the boat forward, turns her to the southwest, and puts her up a quarter speed.

The winds which blew up to the predicted 60 miles an hour during the night have subsided to 10 to 15 but the seas whipped by the winds and swelled by the strong tides from the Bay of Fundy are running heavy and once again directly into the path of the *Joseph & Lucia III.* Even at a quarter speed the men are having trouble keeping their balance on deck. Tommy is caught by the urge to go full steam and the recognition that he ought to slow down until the deck is cleared.

For to handle the dogfish and the redfish the men have to stand and cull the fish out with a gaff, and there is not much they can hold on to and the boat is twisting through the uneven waves and the deck is awash with spray and water running through the scuppers. And sometimes the rails are nearly buried under the waves, the boat lists so far over, and the fish slide across the pen, then back, and the men reach out for the wires or the edge of the checkerboards or the mast or the gallows frames to keep from pitching headfirst into the mess on deck or falling back against the rail.

And as the men fight for balance they are grabbing into the mess of fish and snatching dogfish by the tails or the neck and tossing them overboard—with a vengence. The dogfish are wrapped around each other like pick up sticks and often have to be tugged free with two hands, and frequently they come loose with the trail of a smaller fish snapped in their sharp-teethed mouths. And there is an unrepentant glaze in their eyes as though they know that no matter how the fishermen hate them, all the men can do is toss them overboard to swim away to eat more fish in

more nets. And to procreate, for the dogfish is the rabbit of
the ocean.

In his frustration Tommy grabs the CB set speaker off
the hook over his head and practically yells.

"Nino . . . come in, Nino," and waits, holding the
speaker in his left hand which he rests on the gear. There's
no answer.

"Nino . . . come in, Nino." Again no answer. He hangs
the speaker up and leans back in his stool and watches the
work on deck.

*Oh, my Gawd, Tommy. Rimwrack, Tommy. You
should see. You wouldn't believe . . ."*

*Yah, Nino, we got problems here, too. Dogfish. Some
redfish, but dogfish all over the deck . . .*

*Oh, my Gawd, Tommy, we got three hours' work ahead
of us. Three hours, Tommy. We won't get another set in
today, I don't think . . .*

*Yah, I guess not, Nino. Wha'd'ya got—3:30, yah, Nino,
it'll be dark before you got that net ready . . . yah, well,
we're steaming. I don't see staying around here for the
dogfish. Jesus Christ, Nino, I made a mistake. Shoulda come
here first, found there was dogfish, and gone to Southwest
Bank for the haddock. I'da had a trip and come down to
you. Now I've lost a day . . .*

*Yeah, well, Tommy, there's company down here. I
don't know. I been catching good. A few thousand cod last
set before we rimwracked, but I don't know, Tommy,
all these boats here. They're breaking the fish up pretty
good . . .*

*What'm I going to do? If I go back to southwest I'm
going to get haddock. What'm I going to do with more*

*haddock? Give 'em to you? I got too much now. I try to take these out in Boston they'll jump on me faster'n a fly can piss. I stay here, I got a trip of dogfish. I gotta come down, Nino. Look around. It's no good, maybe I'll go down offa Cape Cod. I don't know, I gotta do something. I can't go in with what I got . . .*

*Yah, well, Tommy, you do what you gotta do. I'm just telling you. I mean, you gotta see, so see. We got a few fish, you might as well come . . .*

*Yah, well, O.K., Nino. We started half an hour ago. The boys are still on deck, but they'll be off soon now . . . we got a fucking headwind again. Everywhere we go we got a headwind this trip. What's the weather by you?*

*Fifteen . . . twenty, but it was bad last night outa the southwest. You'll be coming straight at it . . .*

*What are you going to do? I guess we'll be there by morning . . . see you then . . .*

*O.K., Tommy, see you when you get here. Yah . . .*

Tommy hangs the speaker back up. On deck, the last of the redfish are being shoveled through the bunker plate on deck and into the pens in the hold set aside for the redfish. Santo stands by the winch, Joe Charley hooks the long gilson into the splitting strap of the cod end, and Santo lifts it up. The men push and tug it across the deck and lay it between the checkerboards over the net packed along the rail. Except for battening the gear down, the work is done, and Tommy pushes the throttle all the way forward and the boat lurches southwest toward Jeffreys Ledge.

And a wave immediately crashes over the bow and like a flash storm soaks the crew as they tie the net in place. Gil looks up toward the pilot house. The rest continue working.

* * *

## LOG—WEDNESDAY

7:30 A.M.  Off Jeffreys Ledge

7:50 A.M.  Set out

8:10 A.M.  Breakfast: fried eggs, bacon, toast, oranges, coffee

11:30 A.M.  Haul back: some cod and pollock

1:00 P.M.  Lunch: meat loaf, canned beans, canned pears

2:30 P.M.  Haul back: cod and pollock. Brought a scup up in the net. The scup is a southern-water fish. Gil held it up for Tommy to see: "There's something wrong with your compass, Cap."

3:00 P.M.  Set out: seas picking up—winds 30–35 mph

5:10 P.M.  Haul back: parted ground wire; some damage, mending

6:30 P.M.  Set out

8:00 P.M.  Supper: fried hake, cabbage, canned peaches, coffee

11:00 P.M.  Haul back: *six* fish, net back on board

11:10 P.M.  Jog to the eastward

1:30 A.M.  Stop and drift, to westward: winds 35–40 mph

* * *

Nino was right. There's too much company on Jeffreys Ledge and no fish left. They've scattered into the shoaler waters and it's taking a chance going in after them, what there are left of them, that is.

And for the second straight tow the net lies on deck, only this time rimwracked good, in shreds, the belly torn right out of it, huge slices through the wings. It's the same problem that beset Nino two days earlier. It's already nearly six o'clock in the evening, the sun has already set,

the gray is turning black, and the fish are about to rise off
the bottom into midwater.

"Oh, my Gawd," Tommy moans in the pilot house.
"Oh, my Gawd! If I hadn'a had a phone I'da done all right.
I'da stayed where I was and made a trip and wouldn'a
listened to that fucking Nino and come down here. This is
small-boat grounds. We shouldn't be fishing here, but what
ya going to do? Where there's fish, you gotta go where they
are, but what we got now is the trash."

"Shouldn'a gone in there, Cap . . ." It's Santo Mineo of
the *Antonina* on the CB set:

*I tol' ya, that's bad bottom in there. We can't drag
through that . . ..*

*What're you telling me? I know. I got the friggin' net
on deck again, but where else am I going to go? You guys
busted up the fish. I gotta go after 'em . . .*

*That's right, Cap. We're not catching nothin' either. I
don't know, Tommy. I think we'll be going in, take a chance
on tomorrow's market. I heard the* Santa Maria *got a good
price today. Who knows? There's nothing here now . . .*

*Yah, that's right. That's right. But we go in, no one gets
a price. You go in, we gotta stay out . . . an' we gotta stay
out anyway. We haven't got a trip yet. We'll see what's
around, give 'em a night. Maybe there'll be something tomorrow . . .*

*Yeah, well, okay, Cap. Maybe we'll see you. I don't
know. I hate going in if there's no price, but we'll
see . . .*

*Okay . . . okay . . .*

But even as Tommy is maundering he's made up his
mind, and he opens the window and yells down, "Go on and

eat. Do that after. We're steaming." To Sharrers Ridge near Fipennies Ledge, eight hours east-by-southeast, after redfish—that were there two years ago.

Supper is leftovers: warmed up meat loaf, a couple of pieces of fried chicken, some cold haddock, fried potatoes, coffee or canned cold drinks, and cheese. Gil is suffering from a lapse of enthusiasm. Unspoken is the awareness that other boats are going in and that home is only forty miles away. It's one thing to be 180 miles from a warm bed, but forty miles is like sitting in the driveway—and being locked in the car.

And the boat has been six days out.

And there is only one can of ginger ale left. It's sitting in front of Gaspare, unopened. Not actually in front, but closer to Gaspare than it is to Joe Charley, who reaches a long way across the table and grabs it—and opens it quickly and begins to sip from it.

Which makes Gaspare mad because he coveted that can of ginger ale and had made certain before he sat down for supper—and he sat down before the others to insure his certainty—that the can would be within his grasp. And now it is gone to Joe Charley and the suppressed enmity of the "greaser" for the "loud-mouthed bastard" which is shared equally by the "loud-mouthed bastard" for the "greaser" comes out.

And Gaspare, his unshaven face now drawn tight in anger, yells at Joe Charley in a fluid mixture of Italian and English which can only be understood by someone who knows beforehand what the hell he's talking about.

And that is Joe Charley who goes, "Now, now, poor Gaspare, lost his little ginger ale, has he? Well, now, ain't that just too bad."

Which has the effect of reducing Gaspare to bitter Sicilian, only a portion of which Joe Charley understands. But Joe Charley has made a reputation for himself, both on board and ashore, for taking nothing from anyone. (He once knocked a Registry of Motor Vehicles officer cold for stopping him while speeding . . . and beat the resulting charge of assault and battery on a police officer by claiming the officer called him a "fucking guinea.")

"You want one so bad, go get it yourself, you fucking cry baby," Joe Charley says.

"I got it and you have it," Gaspare spits back, his English having curiously returned to him.

"Go fuck yourself," says Joe Charley, taking a long sip.

"Botha youse, shut up." Tommy is fed up at this point, he doesn't care if the men kill themselves, but not while he's eating and not while he's worrying about getting his trip. "I don't need this shit on board this boat. Whoever's got the g'damned thing, drink it; the other one get another one. What a bunch of fucking babies! Jesus Christ!" And he goes back to his fried chicken. Both Gaspare and Joe Charley stare down at their plates. Tony grabs an orange and begins peeling it with great concentration while Gil sits down on the edge of the bench next to Tommy and quietly gazes at the stove.

* * *

On Friday there are seven sets, the first at 1:30 in the morning. It is snowing then and the wind is blowing at 25 mph and the weather report calls for gales before the day is out.

At 1:30 P.M. the *Joseph & Lucia III* hauls back part of a wreck, one that is not marked on the chart which resembles a graveyard for all the crosses denoting wrecks in the area.

At 10:45 A.M. the three-hour tow returns a few redfish, more pollock, and a bottle of compressed gas which is leaking and threatens to blow up any moment and is quickly heaved overboard.

At two in the afternoon, no redfish, but a few hundred pounds of hake and a net of dogfish.

And Tommy puts on a tape featuring a comedy routine about an Italian who comes to America and instantly finds himself in trouble for being the pleasant-natured dupe he is. Tommy offers his own translation as the tape plays and forgets for the moment that he is in the midst of his third wasted day and the trip may not be made:

"This guy, he has a car, right? And he stop like he's supposed at a red light and this broad, she bump into his back end. Now he's just from the old country and he don't speak English too good and along comes this cop. So this guy thinks everything's going to be okay, right? But the cop, he's an Irish, and the girl, she's an Irish, too, and not only she's Irish but she's got a set a bumpers . . . [Tommy gives his idea of how impressive her bumpers are] . . . and so now this guy's in trouble 'cause the cop's Irish and so's the girl and she's got these bumpers and the cop's accusing him of stopping too fast and causing an accident . . . and he says it's 'cause there was a red light and now the cop's accusing him of talking back to a police officer . . . and now the cop's taking him off to jail . . ."

Tommy likes the song so much he has to repeat it when Tony comes up from the deck, forgetting that it has been blaring out over the deck while the men were clearing out the dogfish and dressing down the hake. And Tony smiles quietly and sits down on the port stool, picks up a Radio Shack catalogue, and begins thumbing through it.

And at 6:00 P.M. Tommy sets out and begins to tow

toward Roger's Swell, an hour to the eastward. It's been a bad day. No redfish.

And the weather report calls for winds 35 to 40 mph from the southeast, switching during the night to 35 to 40 from the northwest, which means that whichever way the tow goes there is no escape. And the winds are predicted to bring snow and freezing temperatures.

Tommy puts on the DiMara sisters again and leans back in his stool to study the fishscope.

* * *

It's Saturday morning and the crew is beginning to guess when Tommy plans to head in. Everyone knows the boat's been out a week and there is no trip on board, and the way the fish have been running it might be another week before they have enough, if then.

Gil figures Monday morning, because that's what he overheard Tommy tell Tina seven days ago.

"No way," says Joe Charley. "He'll go back to Jeffreys tonight for groundfish."

"He don't want Monday's market," says Gil. "He'll figure there'll be too many boats in over the weekend and the price won't be no good. He'll go in Monday, take out Tuesday morning."

"Tuesday morning," says Santo. "He's got an appointment with the doctor, Thursday. Take out Wednesday."

"He might go in tonight," Joe Charley offers. "Nino's been bellyaching, wants to go in. When Nino goes, he'll go."

"Shit. Nino's been wanting to go in for the last three days. Nino won't go in till he says it's time," Gil says.

"I ask him maybe he's asked the Coast Guard to fly out some food," says Santo. "He say, 'What's wrong with sea gull?' "

"Funny man," says Gil. "All I know's I got food enough for three more days, then it's spaghetti and baked beans, boys."

Seven-thirty in the evening. Hung up. Light rain. The crew open pocketknives, get out whetstones, get out needles, get out twine, spread out the net, pick out holes, start to mend. Slowly. Silently. Wearily.

Tommy, leaning out the window, watching, says something. No one hears. No one looks up. All working.

"I said, 'Put it on board.' We're going home."

The crew stands up, stares at him.

"Finish it and put it away, that's it." He pulls up the window and takes down the speaker for the CB set. To tell Nino.

There is a quiet cheer. No more. Santo goes to the winch, frees the long gilson . . .

# 7

---

# *Going In*

**T**ommy has a memory, one of his many such memories from his youth, about the donkeys in Sicily. He says, "The jackass, he know the way home. You point him, you no stop him. No-o-o-o way."

And "you no stop" the *Joseph & Lucia III,* or the *Joseph & Lucia II,* fast on her stern. Yet, as the boats plow homeward through the black flatness across the undefined, unending, horizonless sea, they seem to labor against invisible reins. They lurch, bull, plunge, but never seem to be any further ahead than they were when they were turned westward for port. Or so it seems.

And it seems that way because of what the fishermen call "channel fever." Anyone who has been away from home for any length of time knows "channel fever": the restlessness, the impatience, the questions about what has gone on since they've been away, the mental pictures of people and places so personal, so missed (if not actually thought about) that develop coupled with the delicious— or in some cases worrisome or anxious—realization that in a matter of time—and the hours and the minutes can be counted—they will cease to be pictures and will, almost as in a fairytale, become the things themselves.

Yet it takes so long. It is still eight hours—a regular workday—until land falls. And after awhile the anticipation wears thin and the anger in frustration at the boat that won't go any faster cloys, and massive, wearying boredom descends and a sense of purposelessness intrudes, a feeling of having nothing to do, of being somewhere between two worlds which is almost the same as being nowhere intrudes, and the men resign themselves to plodding, bucking ten knots an hour through a trackless sea over which a blanket of rain is heavily falling.

And Tommy sleeps. And Tony sleeps. And Gil sleeps. And Gaspare keeps his two-hour watch while Santo and Joe Charley sleep. Then Santo holds his watch while Gaspare and Joe Charley sleep. Then Joe Charley takes the watch and Santo returns forward to sleep, and that's six hours down, and finally Gaspare resumes his watch. And the bright-green numbers on the Loran C tick on and off, changing now and then, telling anyone who wants to read them that landfall is nearing and nearing . . .

And in the distance a flicker of light low on the water, then more lights. And Tommy, without being told, comes from his black cabin aft up the four steps to the black chart room to stand in the doorway of the lightless pilot house, holding fast to the jambs, leans in and says, "Thacher's."

Then in the dark, he feels for a tape along the shelf over the chart table and sticks it in the tape deck. And Italian torch music fills the pilot house and Tommy comes in and takes his stool and swivels around so he's looking toward the wheel and he begins to explain.

"He say, "Without you I must die, for your love is the food of my heart.' And she say, 'No one die for love. You are stupid.' And he say, 'I no care what you say, I am dying, for you are going away.' And she say, 'I don't care, for I love another many.' "

And he begins to laugh.

"She's some bitch, eh? Eh? He says he's dying and all the time she's making it with some other guy. He's a jackass, that's what I think, He's dying because he not going to lay her no more, but she not worried 'bout that. She getting all she want.

"I think she's right. He's stupid."

Then Tommy reaches for the CB speaker:

*Hey, Nino. How you getting home? You call Nina?*

*Nah, Tommy, one of the boys says he's got a car. I don't want to wake her. My Gawd, it's three o'clock.*

*What you got that woman for, you don't call her to pick you up? What's she doing now that's so important? Sleeping. She's been sleeping since you been away. You call her . . .*

*Tommy, I can't do that. You call Tina. You take me home . . .*

*Yah, I call Tina. A fifteen-minute walk and I'm going to call Tina to come get me. You outa your fucking mind?*

*I don't know, Tommy. Sometimes I gotta wonder . . . where we gonna tie up? Rogers Street?*

*I guess so. Won't be no one going out tomorrow anyway. Monday we go to Boston. Might as well . . .*

*Yeah, Tommy, that's what I'm thinking. Well, I gotta go clean up. I'll see you in there . . .*

*I'm waiting to get home before I clean up. Nice warm bath, warm sheets. I'm telling you . . .*

*That's right, Cap, that's right. I'll see you . . .*
*Okay, Nino . . .*

And he hangs up the speaker. "Better call the crew.
There's the breakwater," he says to Gaspare.

And it is the breakwater, blacker on the black water.
And the Eastern Point lighthouse. And scattered lights
along the back shore. And off the starboard the whistler
buoy, then hard starboard and in past the breakwater to the
calm outer harbor. Ahead, the soft glow of a sleeping city
and the line of street lights along Stacey Boulevard on
which no cars are yet driving. And the flashing red light of
Ten Pound Island. And Curcuru's to port and Rocky Neck
to starboard, and straight ahead the lights of the Coast
Guard station, and after it the long wharf of the Gloucester
Marine Railways on Rogers Street.

And the men come on deck and take their stations and
slowly the boat settles back to a trawl, then coasts out of
gear, and there is a rush of the engines in reverse and the
*Joseph & Lucia III* slides alongside the pilings. Joe Charley
runs up the wood ladder to catch the lines thrown first by
Santo, then by Gaspare, and lays them around bollards.
And the boat comes to a halt. And the engines stop and
there is, for the first time in eight days, complete silence.

One after the other the men, bags under their arms,
climb the ladder and start down the wharf. Tommy and Joe
Charley walk together. It is cold, but the rain has stopped
and, where the streetlights glow, the city shows clean and
slick. No one says good-bye because there is no "good-bye"
to it. The workday is over; the men are going home. It is
as simple as that. They have the rest of the day off and at
3 A.M., Monday morning, they will be back on board to

bring the boat to Boston to sell the fish.

Tommy and Joe Charley walk up the wharf to Harbor Loop and around by Empire Fish Co. and the Building Center, and across Rogers Street and up Duncan Street by the ruins of the old police station, across Main Street by Sterling Drug Store, up Pleasant Street and cut across the municipal parking lot toward City Hall, then through the old playground of the abandoned Central Grammar School, and by the Fire Barn and up School Street, past the house where Tommy's daughter and Joe Charley's sister Lucy and her family lie sleeping, and across Prospect Street to the corner of Addison Street and School Street where Tommy says, "I guess I'll just go down here to the house in the southwest corner."

And Joe Charley says he'll be by to see Momma in the morning, and goes one more block and takes a left up Pearl Street to the last house on the left and lets himself into the first apartment, where his wife and two-year-old daughter lie sound asleep.

# 8

## *Settling the Trip*

*I*t's agreed, this trip Tommy will go to Boston and sell his
fish first, and Nino will come down the next day. Neither
of them has a good trip on board, but together they have
enough to glut the market on the Boston Fish Pier.

It wasn't always that way. Even a decade ago, the boats
might be tied two deep along the pier waiting to take out
their fish, and the fish dealers with their many processing
stalls side by side up and down the long pier would be
fighting among each other for a piece of the catch.

But no more. The bulk of the fish that are processed
now on the Boston Fish Pier comes over the road in refrigerated trucks from Canada, and what few boats that still
take out in Boston vie with one another for that dwindling
percentage of locally caught fish the dealers will buy.

Not that the dealers won't buy all Tommy and Nino can
bring in. They will, eagerly, and stockpile it for a leaner day.
But they won't give much of a price and the boats won't
make any money, and later the dealers will sell the fish at
top dollar and pocket the difference; and neither Tommy
nor Nino feel like working a week to two weeks in 35-mile-
an-hour winter winds, in snow and ice and heaving seas,

twenty-four hours a day, to provide windfalls for the dealers.

Yet coming down separately is still taking a chance. Just because Nino is holding over a day is no guarantee that Tommy will get top dollar for his fish. All it takes is the big stern trawler *Tremont* out of Boston to be in with 80,000 pounds of fish to drop the bottom out of the price. And there is no knowing where the *Tremont* is . . .

And Tommy can't hold over another day because that's Nino's turn, and if he waits a third day that will mean four days in port that he's not fishing, with a fifth day for supplying the boat with ice and fuel and grub, and there's some electronic work to be done and that might mean a sixth day before he can go out again—nearly a week that the net will not be overboard, that fish will not be caught, that no one will be making any money.

As always in fishing there's the gamble. The trip started with a hunch on a "big killing" of gray sole and it cost a day to steam to Grand Manan Banks to find there were no gray sole, but haddock instead. Too much haddock. And where the redfish were supposed to be there were dogfish. And that cost a day. And it was another day lost steaming all the way back to Jeffreys Ledge, only to find that what fish had been there were scattered by the other boats and the grounds were barren and that was another two days, one with practically nothing to show. Then the chance that there might be redfish off Sharrers Ridge had not come through. It was all chance. The odds were at best fifty-fifty and there was always the possibility that, badly as things were going, there would be that one lucky set on a thick school of cod or pollock and in two days there might be eighty thousand pounds of fish in the hold. (Three trips later this would happen.)

But as the *Joseph & Lucia III* steams slowly through the black of early-morning night into Boston Harbor, Tommy knows that the lucky set is no longer possible. He has forty thousand pounds of fish in the hold. That's all. Forty thousand pounds in a hold designed for three times that amount, and all he can hope for now is that there are no other boats in and that the freezers on the pier are not filled with Canadian fish and the dealers are in a buying mood.

If ever there was a fish out of water, it is Tommy Brancaleone on the Boston Fish Pier. As he navigates through the myriad of small islands that dot the entrance to Boston Harbor, he grows more and more taciturn. Even his beloved tapes, to which he has turned so often during the long, wearying days fishing, are in the rack and instead the radio is on with news of the world and a kind of Muzak between the newscasts. And he scarcely says a word as he intently studies the radar, fiddling with the knobs to bring the islands into contrast. And he barks directions to Santo, who sits by the automatic pilot as the boat weaves its course past the dark bulks of rock and grass, first to port, then to starboard, and the outline of the harbor takes its shape on the radar screen and comes closer and closer. And far off to the starboard is the half-arc of lights of the Mystic River Bridge, and closer to starboard the runway lights of Logan Airport, and a point off the starboard bow in the gradually lightening sky the bare outline of the spine of high-rise buildings up the center of Boston, and before the boat are the lights of the South Boston Naval Shipyards. And passing off to port an empty tanker and more islands. Then the *Joseph & Lucia III* reaches the main channel and turns to starboard and heads toward the low bank of lights ahead.

And Tommy turns off the radar and tells Santo to go forward and call the men.

The closer the boat gets to the lights, the harder Tommy stares ahead until at last he can see the outline of the Boston Fish Pier, a long, black, unbroken line of two-story buildings running out into the harbor, and at the end the single two-story building that is the Fish Exchange—and at the end of the pier a large boat. The *Tremont.*

"I'll be a sonavabitch" is all Tommy says. And stands up and leans against the shelf by the wheel. And the Muzak keeps droning.

It is 6:15 A.M. and, while it is still dark, night has passed and somewhere at sea to the east someone is watching the sun rising. And in an hour the sky will be a dark blue and the row of fish stores along the pier will lose their back-alley gloom and will take on their sooted, deep-brown brick hue, and the snow on the cement pavement will become gray-white, and the lights in the lumpers' lounge on the first floor of the Exchange building will go out, or seem to, and the harbor will turn a cold, cold blue, and the planes will take off sparkling silver from Logan Airport out over the islands, bending upward over the city or out to sea. And the noise of the city, of the trucks rumbling along the cobblestones of Northern Avenue and the sound of construction at the South Station complex . . . and closer, the sound of the small tractors hauling the fish away in carts and the roar of the winch engine as the baskets are lowered into the holds and filled by the lumpers beneath and raised and swung to the pier and dumped. And the talk, the constant chatter and the yelling and the comaraderie of workmen working at mindlessly repetitive, yet rough and ready jobs.

But for the moment the *Joseph & Lucia III* sits tied to the pier and below the crew eats breakfast while Tommy, nervous, finds little things to do in the pilot house, straightening this, putting that there, and often just standing, looking out over the deck, then over at the Fish Exchange, then at the clock, then picking up a paper towel and cleaning off the top of the radar. Even the radio is off.

And a man walks lazily across the lot between the boat and the Fish Exchange and stops at the edge of the pier by the bow, stands there a moment surveying the boat, then tries to step across the gap between the two. But the tide is down and the boat swings too far from the pier, so he walks down the length of the boat again to stand, still looking up at the port window of the pilot house and calls, "Tommy. Hey, Cap! Hey, anyone in there?"

Tommy hears him, mumbles "Go fuck yourself," and continues fidgeting about the pilot house.

"Hey, Capt'n Tommy, I wanta tell you somping."

Tommy takes a deep breath and goes to the port window, pulls it down, and growls, "What the fuck you want, you can't wait till seven?"

"Now, Tommy, hold your horses. Take it easy, for Christ sake. All I want to know is, you be willing to go with two booms. Just you and the *Tremont*. Two booms we get you out quick."

"No, I don't want no two booms. What I want two booms for? I don't have enough fish for two booms."

"How much you got?"

"How should I know? I ain't got it figured yet. I'll know at seven."

"Well, I thought I'd ask. I don't care when youse boys

get home. I just figured you'd want t'see your old lady sooner. I don't give no shit."

"Don't do me no favors, Vito. You just make sure you do your job. I'll do mine."

"O.K., Tommy. Okay. As I say, I don't give a shit neither way." And he walks back toward the Fish Exchange.

And Tommy shuts the window. "The cocksucker," he grumbles. "Two booms. Who's he think we are? One boom and he's got us paying for six men. Six men! Four's more'n they need. And now he wants us to pay six more men. Jesus Christ! Isn't there anybody 'round here ain't got his hand out. Forty bucks a man for five hours work and he wants two booms."

Tommy takes a small piece of scrap paper out of his breast pocket, lays it on the shelf, turns on the light in the pilot house, gets out a pencil, and studies the figures on the paper. He makes some corrections, then puts the pencil down, tucks the piece of paper back in his pocket, turns off the light, and gets into the tan parka hanging on the back of his swivel stool. He finds his red knit cap on the shelf, pulls it on, goes to the port door, tugs it open, and leaves. He descends the ladder, then climbs up on the rail, poises for a moment, then leaps for the pier, hauls his fifty-four-year-old body up over the edge, stands up, and walks slowly, hands in pockets, toward the Fish Exchange.

The Fish Exchange building is made of granite with small columns on either side of the front door. It stands at the butt end of the pier, unattached to either of the two rows of fish stalls that run down the length of the pier toward Northern Avenue. It has the thick-necked, heavy-browed, worn, and careless, slightly shabby look of someone who has seen about all there is to see of the carryings-on of men and can no longer be surprised or excited. Which is a reasonable description of the men who have already gathered inside waiting for the exchange to open and the selling to begin.

They mill around a large wood platform with time-polished mahogany rails on all sides set in the middle of a broad, high-ceilinged room. On one side of the room is a row of what might be post office or cashier windows, all closed, with no obvious signs of ever opening again. On the other side is a wide anteroom with small offices opening into it and dark-wood railroad-waiting-room benches along the wall and a bulletin board filled with yellowing official releases. And an unkempt men's room off the far corner.

Where the anteroom ties into the main room there is a wall covered by a huge green blackboard blocked off with white lines. A number of men stand around an old man with horn-rimmed glasses who is laboriously writing out the hail for the *Tremont,* breaking down the 88,600 pounds of mixed fish into species: 12,000 pounds of scrod cod, 8,000 pounds of haddock, 1,500 pounds of cusk, 4,000 pounds of hake, and so on.

Tommy comes in through the main doors, quietly pushes by a bunch of lumpers already dressed heavily in sweatshirts, wool jackets, torn and foul oilskins, some with their hardhats on, some with them tucked under their arms, all of whom, not at all quietly, are helping one of their number tell how he hit at Suffolk Downs, Saturday afternoon. Before their loudness Tommy seems to diminish, certainly to shy away.

He walks across the room to the old man by the blackboard and gives him the slip from his shirt pocket.

"Where's that brother of yours?" the old man asks. "I

can't believe I see you here without him. I didn't think youse two dared to go anywhere without the other."

"He'll be coming tomorrow," Tommy mumbles and edges away.

"Is that right? What kinda trip he got?" the old man asks.

"How the fuck should I know?" Tommy growls, and in backing away runs his eye over the *Tremont*'s hail, then turns around and finds a place in the far side of the room just in front of the closed windows. And stands there, waiting.

The room is painted pea green, dull, dirty, and the high ceiling once was white. And the air already so early in the morning is stuffy with cigar and cigarette smoke and the smell of cheap coffee. There is a din of mumble, mumble, mumble as the dealers come in, some singly, others in pairs, and float between one another, saying good morning in that way of competitors who have lived beside each other for years, and in some cases, generations, and who will, in a matter of minutes, join the daily ritual of battle—or might not join the battle if some deal can be made beforehand. For this is their day. There is too much fish; they can do what they want with the price. There is no compulsion to buy unless they can see a real profit. And so there is a lot of whispering, of forming groups and breaking from them, of taking someone aside and talking earnestly, and nodding, and counternodding, and shaking of heads in some sort of understanding and then going separate ways.

And Tommy waits in the back, watching, listening, feeling a growing disgust and discouragement, for it's his fish that's being whispered about, that's being bargained for even before it goes up for auction. And almost without anyone noticing, three men climb up the three stairs onto the platform in the center of the room, walk to the front facing the closed windows, find microphones which they carefully tie around their necks, and, while they are preparing themselves, a voice comes over the public address system: "All nonmembers—out . . . all nonmembers—out," and the lumpers, in no particular hurry, wander toward the door and stand in the doorway shouting to one another, and the voice comes back: "All nonmembers—out . . ." and before the voice is finished, one of the men on the platform begins.

"Four thousand cod scrod from the *Lucia.* What've I got for the scrod, what've I got . . ." and as he wonders what he's got for the scrod, the second man is calling for bids on "four thousand hake. *Tremont* . . . four thousand hake. *Tremont* . . ."

And lost in the din is "twenty-five dollars" for the scrod cod, and the man nods: "Twenty-five dollars. Do I hear thirty? Do I hear thirty? . . . Twenty-six for the scrod. Twenty-six. Do I hear twenty-seven. Twenty-seven . . ." and he waits, looking around, studying faces, knowing from experience who will be the bidders for what, who might go higher, what the ceiling is going to be due to the Canadian fish. And the hake is at twenty-three dollars, and all the time the dealers are wandering back and forth among each other still chatting, still whispering, and once in awhile one will look up at the auctioneers and nod and the auctioneer will nod and the price will go up a dollar and someone will yell, "A share," and the auctioneer will look around and another dealer will nod and the auctioneer will say, "Two shares at twenty-seven . . . three shares" in response to another nod. "Four shares . . . ?" and will wait and someone will say, "Twenty-eight," and the auctioneer will repeat: "Twenty-eight for the scrod . . ." and there will be no answer and suddenly the price will be back down to twenty-seven dollars for the scrod and that's because the twenty-eight bidder found that no one wanted to buy scrod with him at twenty-eight cents, that is, no one wanted a share of four thousand, and he didn't want the entire batch, so he withdrew his bid and settled for a share at twenty-seven.

And all the time Tommy is looking more and more glum and beginning to pace back and forth, and one of the bigger dealers, a man named Vito, comes up to him and says, "It's okay, Cap. We'll take care of you. We'll give you the best price we can," and he seems genuinely concerned, and in a way he is because he still counts on Tommy to catch fish and he doesn't want Tommy to decide to take out his fish in Gloucester. Which is the alternative Tommy is considering and which he spits back at Vito.

"That's no good, Tommy. No way you're going to get a price in Gloucester. They gotta be lower than we are. They gotta be. They gotta pass their fish through here anyway. They can't deal like we can. They ain't got quantity. You know that, Tommy. Don't talk so foolish. We're good to you."

"You're good to me!" Tommy gives Vito his astounded and confused look. "You're good to me? I gotta laugh. That's good? Twenty-seven for scrod? You know it's gotta be at least thirty. Why do I go fishing for twenty-seven. It don't pay the grub bill."

"Tommy, we do what we can for you. Trust me."

"I don't trust nobody," says Tommy, and Vito shrugs.

"You won't do no better in Gloucester. You know that," Vito says.

"I don't know. I gotta figure. Maybe next trip . . . I don't know."

"You figure it, Tommy. You'll be back," and Vito walks

off to another whispering session. And Tommy watches him go and stares at Vito's tan face. For Vito just got back from two weeks in Bermuda.

And on it goes as it always has, although not half as fiercely because it is no longer a two-way street. It's a buyer's market for good. And while the price is better than it was ten years ago, even five years ago, the fishermen are no longer in a position of any strength. They simply do not have the numbers, either in boats or in fish. It is a matter of time before the Boston Fish Pier will exist solely on imported Canadian fish, and that is something the dealers don't want to see happen anymore than the fishermen do. For as long as there are boats like the two *Joseph & Lucia* s and the *Tremont* and the *Old Colony,* each capable of landing seventy thousand to eighty thousand pounds of fish every two weeks, the Canadians are obliged to remain competitive. Without the boats as a buffer, the Canadians will be able to dictate the price to Boston and the profit margin for the dealers will have to taper off. Which makes mortgages and Bermuda vacations a little less easy to maintain simultaneously.

". . . Scrod twenty-seven—four shares . . . twenty-seven . . ." the auctioneer waits, waits, looks around, sees no one is paying attention, and calls out, "Eight thousand large cod from the *Lucia* . . . large cod from the *Lucia.* Twenty-eight . . . twenty-eight . . ."

And Tommy, staring grimly down at the floor, sees an empty styrofoam coffee cup lying on its side, takes two steps and kicks it, breaking it down the side, and digs his hands deeper into his pockets, then stares up at the clock over the main doorway which is closed and behind which the lumpers are hanging around, talking loudly and waving their arms, seriously discussing—broads.

And then it is all over and the doors open and the lumpers wander in as the dealers, still mingling, work their way toward their stall, putting the fish cards with the prices and the amounts they—and other dealers—have bought into their hip pockets.

And a tall, rather handsome man named Russel, dressed in a khaki shirt and pants with a gray alpaca vest, and blond, thinning hair bumps on purpose into Tommy, who is still standing by the windows, and says, "Too bad the *Tremont* had to be in, Tommy. Bad kinda luck."

"Bad for me, good for you. I shoulda scratched and gone back to Gloucester," Tommy says.

"Ya never know, Tommy. But what you got to bitch about? You ain't starving, don't give me that shit. I wish I had half what you make each year."

"I give you half, you give me half what you make."

"Now, Tommy, you don't know what we gotta go through. You think we make money. That's what you think. That's what you don't know."

"I know what I know and I know you ain't starving and I know you're breaking my balls."

"And I know I'm going to make Nino a rich man tomorrow, Cap. A rich man, just because you talk the way you do. We take care a you and you don't show no appreciation."

"Oh, go fuck yourself," Tommy grunts and walks out the door and toward the boat. It's an old game—the rules never change.

Outside on the pier, the lumpers have taken over the *Joseph & Lucia III*. Gil, Santo, Gaspare, and Joe Charley are lost among the dozens of heavy, worn, wooden carts that are jumbled as though flung together along the edge of the pier and among the crowd of lumpers, bystanders, and kibbitzers who thread their ways around the carts to mingle and chat and stare onto the deck, where more lumpers stand at the hatches or at the small winch on the bow and yell down at the lumpers in the hold.

And around the periphery men on small tractors scurry back and forth, backing up to attach to the carts and wait to have more carts hitched on until they pull away with the train behind.

And all the time the large canvas basket is being hauled from the hold, fish and ice piled inside, tails and heads hanging over the side, to be swung across the deck to the pier and caught and poured into the carts and sent back across the deck to the hatch and dropped into the hold.

And fish dropping out and falling on the deck or on the pier and being thrown into a corner of the deck or onto a pile of ice on the pier—and mysteriously disappearing among the many hands and bags. And everybody yelling at everyone. And Gaspare, standing aside with Vito the boss lumper, both with pads in their hands, trying to keep track of the fish as they come out of the hold and are hauled away in the train of carts. And Joe Charley, jumping on the end cart of one train and riding with it down the pier, and Santo walking after the next, Gil waiting for a third to fill up, all headed past the huge *Tremont* unloading with the same feverish confusion; onto the small weighing station; and quietly taking their weigh-out stubs from the young clerk seated in the station, a small electric heater at his feet, a Boston *Herald-American* open to the race results on the counter in front of him, both watching the tractor driver calmly get off his machine, walk back to a cart, take two large haddock and return to the tractor, stuff the fish in a bag, then drive off down the pier to one of the stalls where a line of fish cutters wait with razor-sharp knives to render the stiff, frozen fish into fillets . . .

And the morning moves on and the pen boards hauled from the hold grow in stacks along the starboard rail and the men in the hold work without stop because the faster they get the fish out the sooner they'll get out to the bars and the track. And Tommy disappears into the Great Atlantic Fish Co. to talk with Vito. An hour later two large boxes of filleted fish are brought to the boat and laid by the door leading down to the galley, and a half an hour later five large bags of processed shrimp are laid on top of the boxes. And by noon the last basket swings out of the hold and the last cart is driven away.

And like that the pier stands quiet. The tractors are gone, the lumpers are gone. Some carts remain backed in a jumble into each other and the crew sits around the galley table eating leftover chicken and vegetable soup—fresh from a can—and in his corner Gaspare hunches over the table with a pencil, working on the fish count, adding up the weight stubs, checking them against the amounts sold to various dealers at auction, and eating warm Italian bread with slices of cheese.

"What're you telling me now? That cod scrod is twenty-six cents? At 7:30 it's twenty-seven and now it's twenty-six? That's pretty funny, it drops that fast."

Tommy is slouched down in a chair in one of the offices off the lumpers' lounge, and in front of him, bending over a desk, are the white-haired auctioneer named Jimmy, with Vito, Russel, and two other dealers. Their backs are to him. Sitting in another chair beside the desk is Gaspare. He's looking at Tommy with a "what the hell, you can't beat 'em, Cap" look on his face. Jimmy is tallying the count on

a calculator. There are slips spread out around him. Each
of the dealers has slips in his hand and they are all exchang-
ing figures between them.

"Some one of youse crooks going to tell me how that
happens?" The crinkles around Tommy's eyes are furrows
and the muscles in his cheeks are working. His chin is down
on his neck and his hands are deep in his pockets and his
legs are stretched out toward the desk in front of him. He
still has on his red cap.

"You know, Tommy," says Jimmy, without looking up.
"You know . . . we have to spell it out for you? The last
minute they didn't want the scrod at twenty-seven. What'm
I going to do, open the exchange again? I figure twenty-six
is a good price, figuring."

"In a pig's ass," says Tommy. "They don't pull this shit
in Gloucester, you know."

"Take out in Gloucester, then," says Vito. "You won't
come close to twenty-six."

"The *Katy D* got twenty-six last trip—at Empire . . ."

"Yah," says Russel, "and you know what they went for
here? Do you? Thirty! Come on, Tommy. Be smart."

"I'll be smart when I see you later."

"Get off it, Tommy," says Russel, turning around at last
and looking him in the eye. "I bought half your haddock
today. You think I need haddock. I'm full up with haddock,
but I buy anyway so's you don't lose nothing. I get you a
good price and listen to what I get for gratitude . . ."

"You don't lose nothing. Don't you shit me."

"No, I don't lose anything, but I didn't have to buy, I
coulda waited for your brother, but I bought from you.
Now get off it."

"You wanta know something, Tommy." This time it's

Jimmy. "Next time you come in, I'm going to let you take my place. You're going to sell your own fish. You know what'll happen? You'll be lucky you come out with ten dollars. You'll lose your fucking shirt."

"I don't know about that, the way you help me . . ."

"Tommy, what am I going to say? You don't listen to no one. You can't hear reason. You go out and keep fishing, we'll take care of you."

"You'll take care of me. I know that. Twenty-six dollars for scrod, you take care of me, Vito. With friends like you . . ."

But the men are back at the calculator again and they find that Vito received four hundred more pounds of large cod than he thought he was buying.

"Tommy, you let me have the four hundred. Okay?"

"What am I going to do with it? You got it all cut up anyway. How'm I going to get it back now. I don't care."

"That's good, Tommy. I won't forget you." Tommy's eyes close tight for a second, then he looks at Gaspare and returns the "what can you do?" stare.

"Okay, Tommy, the way I figure it, that's $14,621 for the trip," says Jimmy, standing up and pulling all the papers around him into a pile.

"You say so, what can I say?" says Tommy.

"Take care, Old Dog," says Russel, leaving. "You stop worrying or your heart's going to go whacky on you. You gotta watch that heart."

"It'll take more'n you to stop this heart," says Tommy.

"You're such a nice man, Tommy," says Vito, following Russel out the door. "But you gotta learn to recognize your friends."

"I'm looking, I don't see nothing," says Tommy.

"Okay, Cap, I gotta go eat. Why don't you go home?

Don't your old lady want you around no more?" Jimmy says. "See you next trip. Maybe we'll get you better prices."

"With prices like these you won't have to worry. I won't have any boat."

"Come on, Tommy, cry yourself all the way to the bank."

"Yah, whose bank? Your bank or Vito's?"

And Jimmy locks the door behind him. And Tommy walks with Gaspare through the now-empty exchange. They don't say anything to each other.

The day is over. The trip is over. For the first time all day there is music in the pilot house. Tommy feels himself again, the ordeal is done with for another two weeks. He is talking about the time years ago when he was young and the town of Terrisini was scheduled to play a neighboring town in soccer. And this was a very big event and coincided with a fiesta. Only Terrisini's team had hit upon bad times and the way money was being placed in the bars during the afternoons preceding the game, it looked as though the game—and by inclusion, the fiesta—was going to be a debacle. So secretly the powers that could manage such manoeuvres hired a ringer from Palermo for the game, "and he was real tough, you know. He was big, and right away the game starts and he takes the ball right through the scores . . . and the other town, they see what is happening and they get mad and pretty soon there's this big fight and they're all chasing after this guy and he's standing there hitting everyone who comes near him . . . and they have to call in the police . . ."

And on he goes about the game while Tony sits on the port stool listening, nodding every so often when what he hears verges close to the facts, and smiling at the enthusiasm which carries Tommy away from the game, at last. And quietly Tony remembers those days when both he and Tommy would get on their small, two-wheel scooters and push themselves over the narrow, twisting roads to the adjoining towns to watch the soccer games, and when they used to play in the town band for funerals and processions and parades (and he got paid for two because he not only played the clarinet but the soprano saxaphone, which they'd asked him to learn, and once he even filled in for the trumpeter).

And Joe Charley stands between his father and his uncle listening to the story for the how-manyth time, and smiles and thinks about his pigeon coop and about how, one of these days, he's got to stop fishing and about how he's going to see a friend about a construction job.

And on deck Gil appears from the galley with the two garbage pails full of waste which he dumps overboard and then stands by the port rail and watches the boat passing the power plant with the single long chimney in Salem. And there's the marker for Half Way Rock directly amidships and there's Baker's Island off to starboard and directly ahead the cliffs of Magnolia, then Gloucester Harbor. An hour to go. He looks forward to a day free to work on his son's house, knowing that the next day will be spent ordering the grub and storing it and fixing the hot-water container in the galley.

And below, in the forecastle, Santo and Gaspare lie in their bunks, Santo studying a month-old *Stop* as seriously as a lawyer preparing for the bar, Gaspare sleeping, both secure in the certain knowledge that by this time tomorrow they will each have salted another thousand dollars away in the bank.

And back in the pilot house Tommy turns to his brother Tony and says, "We gonna be ready Wednesday?" and Tony answers, "Whenever you say, Cap."